Cook with Aloha
Favorite Recipes from Our 'Ohana to Yours

ISLAND HERITAGE

Cook with Aloha

Published by
ISLAND HERITAGE
P U B L I S H I N G

94-411 Kō'aki Street
Waipahu, Hawai'i 96797
(800) 468-2800
www.islandheritage.com

First Edition, Second Printing, 2003

ISBN 0-89610-132-0

Cover Painting by Zhou Ling

Introduction

If the people of Hawaiʻi were to pick a favorite pastime, it no doubt would be eating. From backyard luʻaus to lavish weddings, from tailgate parties to potlucks at home, food is the centerpiece of just about every Island gathering.

Cook with Aloha is the bible for foodies. On these pages, you'll find recipes for more than 185 tantalizing dishes that will perk up the family table and please even the most finicky guest.

Showcasing the diverse products, seasonings and cooking techniques of Hawaiʻi's cosmopolitan population, the selection includes familiar foods that you've loved from "small kid time" like Banana Bread, Teriyaki Meat Sticks, Barbecue Spareribs, Portuguese Bean Soup, Shoyu Chicken, Stuffed Cabbage, Li Hing Mui Pickled Mango, Malasadas, and Haupia Squares. Adventurous chefs will want to try intriguing options such as Chili Egg Puff, Green Rice, Gulliver's Corn, Popeye's Surprise, Fruit Pizza, Seven Layer Cookies, Puppy Chow and Dirt Cake.

Whatever tempts your taste buds, you'll be happy to know that this cookbook is designed to make your time in the kitchen fun; most of the recipes are simple and easy to prepare. So clear the counters, set out your ingredients and implements, and enjoy both the creative process of cooking and the ʻono (delicious) results!

Measurement Equivalents

3 tsp. = 1 Tbsp.

2 Tbsp. = 1 fluid oz.

4 Tbsp. = 1/4 cup

5 Tbsp. + 1 tsp. = 1/3 cup

8 Tbsp. = 1/2 cup

1/2 cup = 4 fluid oz.

10 Tbsp. + 2 tsp. = 2/3 cup

12 Tbsp. = 3/4 cup

16 Tbsp. = 1 cup

1 cup = 8 fluid oz.

1/4 cup + 2 Tbsp. = 3/8 cup

1/2 cup + 2 Tbsp. = 5/8 cup

3/4 cup + 2 Tbsp. = 7/8 cup

2 cups = 16 fluid oz.

2 cups = 1 pint

2 pints = 1 quart

4 quarts = 1 gallon

Table of Contents

Breads

&

Breakfast

Breads & Breakfast

Awesome Cheese Bread

2 c mayonnaise
1/4 c parmesan cheese, grated
1 fresh garlic clove, minced
1 lg onion, finely chopped
1 lg loaf French or Italian bread, sliced in half lengthwise

Preheat oven to 350°. Mix first 4 ingredients until smooth. Spread onto bread. Put both halves of bread back together and wrap in aluminum foil. Bake for 15 minutes. Open foil and open bread. Broil under broiler until golden brown. Slice and serve.

Baked French Toast

1 sm loaf day-old French bread
3 eggs
3 T sugar
1 t vanilla extract
2 1/4 c milk
1/2 c flour
6 T dark brown sugar
1/2 t ground cinnamon
1/4 c butter
1 c fresh or frozen blueberries

Grease a 9"x13" baking pan. Slice bread diagonally into 1" slices and place in baking dish; set aside. In medium bowl lightly beat eggs, sugar and vanilla. Stir in milk until well blended. Pour mixture over bread in baking dish, turning slices to coat well. Cover and refrigerate overnight. Preheat oven to 375°. In small bowl combine flour, brown sugar and cinnamon. Cut in butter until mixture resembles coarse crumbs. Turn bread slices over in baking dish. Scatter blueberries over bread, and sprinkle evenly with crumb mixture. Bake 40 minutes or until golden brown. Cut into squares to serve.

Cinnamon Coffee Cake

1 box yellow cake mix
2 sm pkgs instant vanilla pudding
4 eggs
3/4 c vegetable oil
3/4 c water
1 t vanilla
1/2 c sugar
1 c pecans, chopped
3 t cinnamon

Preheat oven to 350°. Mix and blend first 6 ingredients. In a separate bowl mix sugar, chopped pecans, and cinnamon. Prepare a 9"x13" pan or Bundt pan with cooking spray. Sprinkle half of chopped pecan mixture onto bottom of pan. Pour half of batter over nut mixture. Add remaining nut mixture, then remaining batter to pan. Bake for 40-45 minutes. Let cake completely cool before removing from pan.

Icing: 2 c powdered sugar
          2-4 T milk

Mix sugar and milk to desired consistency. Drizzle over top of cooled coffee cake.

Delicious 5-Fruit Smoothies

2 lg bananas
1 c frozen mango
1 c frozen strawberries
1/2 papaya
2 c apple juice

Put bananas, frozen mango and frozen strawberries into large blender and blend on medium speed. Add papaya. Pour in apple juice. Blend on high for a minute or two, while mixing with a wooden spoon. Add more juice, if necessary. Pour into 2 large tumblers.

Egg Soufflé

1 lb sausage, cubed
6 eggs
2 c milk
1 c cheddar cheese, grated
1 t dry mustard
1 t salt
6 slices white bread (cut in cubes)

Brown sausage and drain well. In large bowl, beat eggs. Add milk, grated cheese, mustard, salt and bread cubes. Add cooked sausage to egg mixture, mix well. Pour into a buttered 6"x 10" casserole dish. Cover with foil and refrigerate overnight.

Preheat oven to 350°. Bake, covered, for 45 minutes. Remove foil and bake for another 15 minutes, until center is cooked.

Fabulous Corn Bread

2 c Bisquick
3/4 c sugar
4 heaping T cornmeal
1/2 t baking soda
1 c milk
2 eggs, beaten
2 sticks of butter, softened

Preheat oven to 350°. Combine dry ingredients. Set aside. In separate bowl, mix milk, eggs, and butter. Add dry ingredients and mix until blended. Bake for 30 to 40 minutes in greased 9"x9" pan. Test for doneness with toothpick. Double recipe for 9"x13" baking pan.

Famous Kona Inn Banana Bread

        2 c sugar
        1 c butter or margarine, softened
        3 lg eggs
    2 1/2 c flour
        1 t salt
        2 tsp baking soda
        7 overripe bananas, mashed

Preheat oven to 350°. In large mixing bowl cream together the sugar and butter. Add eggs and mix well. Set aside. In separate bowl, combine all dry ingredients. Alternating bananas and dry ingredients, add both to the creamed mixture. Mix only until blended. Lightly grease 2 loaf pans or 1 Bundt pan and dust with flour. Pour batter into prepared pan. Bake for 60 minutes. Test for doneness with a toothpick.

Golden Bran Muffins

    1 1/4 c whole bran cereal
        1 c boiling water
      1/2 c vegetable oil
      3/4 c brown sugar
      1/2 c honey
        2 eggs, lightly beaten
        2 c buttermilk
    2 1/4 c whole wheat flour
    2 1/2 t baking soda
        1 t salt
        2 c granola

Mix bran cereal and water in a large bowl. Set aside for 10 minutes. In another bowl, combine oil, sugar and honey. Add the eggs and buttermilk, beating with a whisk. Stir in the bran mixture. Combine flour, soda, salt and granola. Fold into the other ingredients. Stir slowly. Cover and refrigerate for several hours, or overnight. Preheat oven to 400°. Pour into a lightly greased muffin pan or use paper muffin liners. Bake for 20-25 minutes until golden brown.

Light and Crispy Waffles

- 2 egg yolks
- 2 c milk
- 2 c all-purpose flour
- 1 t baking powder
- 1/2 t salt
- 1/3 c oil
- 2 egg whites, stiffly beaten

Preheat waffle maker. Put all ingredients except egg whites in a large mixing bowl. Beat at low speed until moistened. Increase to medium speed, mix until smooth. By hand, gently fold in beaten egg whites. Pour 1/2 cup batter into waffle maker. Close lid and bake until golden, 2 1/2 to 3 minutes.

Mango Bread

Serves 12-15

- 2 c flour
- 2 t baking soda
- 2 t cinnamon
- 1/2 t salt
- 1 c sugar
- 1/2 c brown sugar, firmly packed
- 3/4 c oil
- 3 eggs
- 2 t vanilla
- Juice of 1 lemon
- 2 c mango, diced
- 1/2 c coconut
- 1/2 c raisins
- 1/2 c dates
- 1/2 c walnuts

Preheat oven to 350°. Sift flour, baking soda, cinnamon and salt together. In a separate bowl, combine sugars, oil, eggs, vanilla, lemon juice and mango. Mix in dry ingredients. Fold in coconut, raisins, dates and nuts. Pour into 2 lightly greased loaf pans or one greased Bundt pan. Bake for 45 minutes until done.

Oven Pancakes

          3 eggs, slightly beaten
       1/2 c flour
       1/4 t salt
       1/2 c milk
          2 T butter or margarine, melted

10-inch skillet, greased (handle must be removable or ovenproof)

Preheat oven to 450°. Slowly add flour to beaten eggs, beating constantly. Stir in salt, milk, and butter. Pour batter into cold pan/skillet. Bake 18 minutes; then reduce heat to 350° and bake 10 minutes longer. May be served with the fruit topping of your choice.

Pamplines (pum-plee-nees)

          1 c flour
          1 c Bisquick
       1/4 c sugar
       3/4 c water
              Flour for work surface

Coating: 1/4 c sugar
              1 t cinnamon

              Paper bag
          1 c oil, for frying

Mix 1 cup flour, Bisquick, sugar and water in bowl. Dust clean work surface with flour. Knead dough. Pull off a small section the size of a large marble and roll between hands until 3 to 4 inches long. Deep fry in oil until golden brown. Drain on paper towel. Combine sugar and cinnamon in paper bag. Drop cooked pampline into paper bag. Shake until well-coated. Serve.

Pumpkin Bread

          4   eggs
        2/3   c water
        3/4   c oil
          1   16oz can pumpkin mix (solid pack)
          2   c sugar
      3 1/3   c flour
          2   t baking soda
      1 1/2   t salt
      1 1/2   t cinnamon
          1   t nutmeg
              Pinch clove powder

Preheat oven to 350°. Beat together eggs, water, oil and pumpkin. Stir in sugar. In a separate bowl combine flour, soda, salt, cinnamon, nutmeg and clove. Add this to egg mixture. Pour into 2 loaf pans and bake 55-60 minutes. Test for doneness with toothpick.

Notes

Starters

Starters

Artichoke Cheese Squares

     2 6oz jars marinated artichoke hearts, drained and chopped
     4 eggs, beaten
    12 crackers, crushed
     8 oz cheddar cheese, shredded
   1/4 c onion, minced
     4 drops Tabasco sauce
   1/2 t garlic powder
        Salt and pepper to taste
1/4-1/2 c parmesan cheese, grated

Preheat oven to 325°. Grease an 8"x8" baking dish using the liquid from artichokes. Combine artichokes, eggs and crackers. Add remaining ingredients except parmesan and mix thoroughly. Pour into baking dish and sprinkle top with parmesan. Bake for 35-40 minutes; cool 5 minutes and cut into 1" squares.

Broccoli Cheese Squares

     3 T butter or margarine
     2 10oz pkgs frozen broccoli
     3 eggs
     1 c flour
     1 c milk
     1 t salt
     1 t baking powder
     1 lb mild cheddar cheese, grated
     2 T onion, finely chopped
        Seasoned salt to taste

Preheat oven to 350°. Melt butter in a 9"x13" baking dish. Steam broccoli until partially cooked, about 5 minutes. Transfer to blender and chop finely. Beat eggs in large bowl. Add flour, milk, salt and baking powder; mix well. Stir in broccoli, cheese, onion and seasoned salt. Spoon into baking dish, spreading evenly. Bake for 30 to 35 minutes. Let stand 5 minutes before slicing into 1" pieces. May be frozen.

Can't Be Beat Spring Rolls

- 2 T oil
- 1 clove garlic, minced
- 1 c carrots, julienne
- 1 c cabbage, thinly sliced
- 1 c canned crab
- 1/2 t salt
- 1 4oz can Pillsbury Crescent Rolls
- 1 egg, beaten for egg wash

Preheat oven to 375°. Add oil in small skillet and sauté garlic and carrots over medium heat for 2 minutes. Add cabbage, crab meat and salt. Stir occasionally for 5 minutes and remove from heat. Unroll crescent rolls into 2" rectangles. Place 1/4 of crab mixture in center of each rectangle. Pinch the long edges and seal to form a roll. Place seam side down on ungreased baking sheet. Brush with egg and bake for 12-17 minutes, or until golden brown. Cut each roll into 4 slices and serve warm.

Cheese Ball

- 1 jar Old English cheese
- 4 oz blue cheese
- 2 8oz pkgs cream cheese
- 2 T onion, minced
- 2 t Worcestershire sauce
- 1/4 c parsley, minced
- 1/2 c pecans, finely chopped

Combine all ingredients except parsley and pecans. Form into one large or two small balls. Combine parsley and pecans. Roll cheese balls in parsley mixture. Chill. Serve with crackers.

Chili Egg Puff

10 eggs
1/2 c flour
1 t baking powder
1/2 t salt
1 pint cottage cheese
1 pound jack cheese, shredded
1/2 c (1 stick) butter, melted

Optional: 2 4oz cans diced green chilies
Sour cream
Salsa

Preheat oven to 350°. Beat the eggs until light and lemon colored. Add flour, baking powder, salt, cottage cheese, jack cheese and melted butter — blending smoothly with electric mixer. Stir in the chilies. (See note below) Pour mixture into a well-buttered 9"x13" baking dish. Bake for 35 minutes until top is golden brown and center appears firm.

Note: To accommodate different tastes, gently add the chilies after putting the mixture in the baking dish and add chilies to only half of the pan. The sour cream and salsa are a nice topping to add individually at the table.

Coconut Chicken Bites

3 1/2 c sweetened shredded coconut
2 lbs boneless skinless chicken breasts, cut into 1" pieces
2 t ground cumin
3/4 t ground coriander
1/2 t cayenne pepper
Salt and freshly ground pepper
2 eggs, beaten
Dijon mustard for dipping

Preheat oven to 325°. Bake coconut on heavy large baking sheet until golden brown, stirring frequently, about 15 minutes. Transfer to bowl and cool. Coarsely grind coconut in batches in food processor

continued...

and place on large plate. Spray 2 heavy large cookie sheets with cooking oil. In a large bowl, combine cumin, coriander, cayenne, salt and pepper. Add chicken pieces, turning to coat. Dip into egg mixture. Dredge chicken pieces in coconut, coating completely. Transfer to prepared sheets. Cover and chill for 1 hour. (Can be prepared one day in advance.) Preheat oven to 400°. Bake chicken until crisp and golden brown, about 15 minutes, turning pieces over once. Arrange chicken on platter. Serve warm or at room temperature with Dijon mustard for dipping.

Serves 6-8

Hot Artichoke Dip

1 14oz can artichoke hearts, drained, chopped
1 c grated parmesan cheese
1 c mayonnaise
Chopped tomato
Sliced green onions

Preheat oven to 350°. Mix all ingredients except tomato and onions. Spoon into 9" pie plate or quiche dish. Bake for 20-25 minutes or until light golden brown. Sprinkle with tomato and onions, if desired. Cook 10 more minutes. Serve with crackers or pita bread triangles.

Serves 12-14

Hot Chicken Wings

2 lbs chicken wings
Salt and pepper to taste

Sauce: 1/2 c soy sauce
6 T sugar
2 cloves garlic, minced
2 green onions, minced
Hot chili sauce, to taste

Brown chicken wings in skillet until done; salt and pepper to taste. Set aside on warm platter. Combine remaining ingredients in a small saucepan and heat to boiling until sugar dissolves. Serve wings with sauce for dipping.

Hot Crab Dip

     2 c mayonnaise
     1 8oz can artichokes (not marinated)
     1 c crab meat or imitation crab meat
    1/2 c fresh parmesan
    1/2 c white or green onion, chopped
    1/4 t Tabasco sauce
     1 t parsley flakes
        Paprika

Mix all ingredients together (except paprika) and spread in 9"x 9" baking or quiche dish. Sprinkle with paprika. Broil 10 minutes before serving or until heated through. Serve with crackers or bread.

Hummus

     2 15 1/2oz cans garbanzo beans
    1/4 c olive oil
     1 T white wine vinegar
    1/4 c yellow onion, coarsely chopped
     2 cloves garlic, coarsely chopped
        Pinch of cayenne pepper
        Salt to taste

Open both cans of garbanzos and drain the juice from one can. Pour the contents of both cans into a food processor and add all other ingredients. Process until very smooth. Serve with pita bread, crackers, cucumber slices or any other kind of vegetables.
Note: For a thicker consistency, drain liquid from both cans.

Kailua Crab Cakes

      1   lb fresh lump crab meat
  1 1/2   c panko flakes
      2   eggs, well beaten
      1   T Dijon mustard
    1/2   t Worcestershire sauce
      2   T parsley, minced
    1/4   c scallions, chopped
      1   t Old Bay seasoning
    1/2   c mayonnaise
           Panko flakes to coat

Place crab meat in a mixing bowl with panko flakes. Add eggs, mustard, and remaining ingredients. Mix gently, leaving the crab lumps as large as possible. Shape mixture into 12-16 equal portions, ball up and flatten into a patty shape about 3/4 to 1" thick. Coat each crab cake with panko flakes. Chill for at least one hour before cooking.

Heat 1/4 c cooking oil over medium heat. Sauté each cake for 2 to 2 1/2 minutes per side in the oil.

*Can yield 4-5 dinner size crab cakes.

Tartar Sauce for Kailua Crab Cakes (makes 1 1/2 cups):
      2   T tarragon vinegar
      1   t Dijon mustard
    1/2   t kosher salt
           Pinch cayenne pepper
    1/3   c cornichons, finely chopped
      1   T shallots, finely chopped
      1   t capers, finely chopped
      1   T leaf parsley, finely chopped
      1   c mayonnaise

Combine ingredients and refrigerate until ready to serve.

Poke

2 lbs fish or tako, chopped
1/4 c chopped ogo
1 clove garlic, chopped
1 t sesame seeds, crushed
1 T oyster sauce
1 T shoyu
1/2 c green onion
1/2 t Hawaiian salt (adjust to taste)
1/2 of a chili pepper
2 t sesame seed oil

Combine all ingredients and toss well. Serve.

Red Bell Pepper and Cheddar Cheese Spread

1/2 small onion, quartered
3 lg garlic cloves, peeled
2 t olive oil
2 lg red bell peppers
1 1/2 c sharp cheddar cheese, grated and well-packed
Dash of cayenne pepper
2 T chopped fresh chives

Preheat oven to 375°. Place onion and garlic in small baking dish. Drizzle with oil. Bake until soft, stirring occasionally, about 50 minutes. Cool.

Meanwhile, charbroil peppers under broiler or over gas flame until blackened on all sides. Cool 10 minutes. Peel and seed peppers; pat dry. Place all ingredients except chives in food processor. Puree until almost smooth. Transfer to bowl. Stir in chives. Season with salt and pepper. Cover and refrigerate at least 2 hours. May be prepared 1 day ahead.

Salmon Balls

    1 lb can red salmon
    1 8oz pkg cream cheese, softened
    1 T lemon juice
    2 T onion, minced
    1 t Worcestershire sauce
 1/4 t salt
 1/4 t liquid smoke
    3 T parsley, chopped

Drain salmon, remove bones and flake. Cream the cream cheese and rest of the ingredients except the parsley. Fold in salmon. Shape into a ball and roll in parsley. Serve with crackers.

Savory Mushroom Cups

Stuffing: 4 T butter
3 shallots, minced
1/2 lb mushrooms, finely chopped
2 T flour
1/2 c heavy cream
3 T fresh or freeze-dried chives, chopped
2 T parsley, chopped
1/2 t salt
1/2 t lemon juice
1/8 t cayenne pepper
24 toast cups (see below)
2 T parmesan cheese, grated

In a large frying pan, melt butter over medium heat. Add shallots and cook until softened but not brown, about 2 minutes. Add mushrooms and cook, stirring occasionally, until nearly all the liquid has cooked away, 10 to 15 minutes. Sprinkle flour over mushroom mixture, and cook, stirring, 2 minutes. Increase heat to high and stir in cream, mixing well. Cook until mixture comes to a boil, about 3 minutes. Remove from heat and stir in chives, parsley, salt, lemon juice, and cayenne. If made in advance, store well-covered in refrigerator up to 3 days.

Toast Cups:
2 T butter, softened
1 lb loaf of thin sliced firm-textured white bread

Preheat oven to 400°. Butter insides of 24 gem-size (1 1/2") muffin tins.

Using a plain or fluted 2 1/2 to 3-inch biscuit cutter, cut a round from each slice of bread and gently press into muffin cups to line bottom and sides. Bake until edges are golden brown, about 10 minutes. Let cool on rack. Store airtight up to 3 days, or freeze.

Preheat oven to 350°. Mound about 1 tablespoon of mushroom mixture in each toast cup and top with 1/4 teaspoon grated parmesan. Bake until tops are golden and mushroom mixture is bubbling hot, about 10 minutes.

Sesame Chicken Wings

      3 lbs chicken wings or drumettes
      2 T flour
    1/4 c cornstarch
    1/4 c mochiko
    1/4 c sugar
      1 t salt
    1/4 c shoyu
      1 T oyster sauce
      2 eggs, beaten
    1/4 c green onions, diced
      2 cloves garlic, crushed
      1 qt peanut oil
      2 c sesame seeds

Disjoint chicken wings. In a large mixing bowl combine flour, cornstarch, mochiko, sugar and salt. Mix in shoyu, oyster sauce, eggs, green onions and garlic. Dip chicken into batter, coating well. Heat oil in large skillet and fry wings until golden. Drain and sprinkle with sesame seeds. Serve warm.

Spinach Balls

      2 10oz pkgs chopped frozen spinach
      4 eggs, beaten
      1 med onion, finely grated
      1 clove garlic, minced
    3/4 c butter, melted
    1/2 c swiss cheese, grated
    1/4 c parmesan cheese, grated
      2 c herb-flavored breadcrumbs

Thaw spinach and drain well. In a large mixing bowl combine spinach and all other ingredients. Mix well. Refrigerate for 2-3 hours. Preheat oven to 375°. Roll into 1" balls. Place on cookie sheet and bake for 10 minutes.

Spinach Rolls

2   10oz boxes frozen spinach, chopped
1   c sour cream
1   c mayonnaise
1/2   c bacon bits
1   pkg ranch dressing
    Green onions, chopped
1/4   c water chestnuts, finely chopped
1   pkg of 10 flour tortillas

Thaw spinach and squeeze until all water is removed. Add next six ingredients–mix well. Spoon mixture onto tortilla, evenly covering 2/3 of the tortilla. Starting with the fullest end, roll up tightly. Carefully cut into slices and serve.

Spinach Triangles

1   pkg Pepperidge Farm Frozen Puff Pastry Sheets (2 sheets)
3   eggs
1   T water
1/2   c crumbled feta cheese
1   pkg (10oz) frozen chopped spinach, thawed and well-drained
1   med onion, finely chopped
2   T chopped fresh parsley

Thaw pastry sheets at room temperature 30 minutes. Preheat oven to 400°. Mix 1 egg with water and set aside for brushing. Mix remaining eggs, cheese, spinach, onion and parsley. Set aside. Unfold pastry on lightly floured surface. Roll each sheet into a 12-inch square and cut each into 16 3-inch squares. Place a tablespoon of spinach mixture in center of each square. Brush edges of squares with egg mixture. Fold squares to form triangles. Press edges to seal. Place 2 inches apart on baking sheet. Brush with egg mixture. Bake 20 minutes or until golden brown. Serve warm or at room temperature.

Sticky Chicken Wings

1/2 c honey
1/4 c catsup
  2 T brown sugar
1/4 c soy sauce
3-4 lbs chicken wings or drummettes

Preheat oven to 350°. Combine first 4 ingredients and mix well. Toss in wings and coat well. Place wings on baking sheet. Bake for about 1 hour, basting 3-4 times.

Teriyaki Meat Sticks

  2 lbs sirloin steak
1/2 c soy sauce
  3 T sugar
  1 T dry sherry
1/2 t minced fresh ginger or
1/8 t powdered ginger
  1 clove garlic, minced

Slice steak diagonally into 2"x1"x 1/4" strips. Combine all the remaining ingredients; marinate meat slices for 30 minutes. Thread slices on skewers. Barbecue or broil until done.

Soups, Salads

&

Dressings

Soups, Salads & Dressings

Broccoli and Raisin Salad

3 c broccoli, chopped
1 c raisins
1 c Spanish peanuts
2 green onions, chopped

Dressing: 1 c mayonnaise
1 T wine vinegar
1 T sugar

Toss all together. Chill and serve. A family favorite!

Broccoli Mandarin Salad

Dressing: 1 egg
1 egg yolk
1/2 c sugar
1 1/2 t corn starch
1 t dry mustard
1/4 c vinegar
1/4 c water
3 T butter
1/2 c mayonnaise

Salad: 4 c broccoli florets, chopped
1/2 c golden raisins
6 slices cooked bacon, crumbled
1/2 c slivered almonds, toasted
1 11oz can mandarin oranges, drained
1/2 c red onion, chopped

In saucepan, mix first 7 ingredients for dressing. Stir over medium heat until thick. Remove from heat. Add butter and mayonnaise, mix well. Chill in refrigerator for 1 hour.

Mix all remaining ingredients. Toss with dressing, chill for 1 hour and serve.

Cherry Cranberry Salad

    1   pkg cherry jello
    1   c boiling water
  1/8   t salt (optional)
    1   can jellied cranberry sauce
    1   c sour cream
    1   c chopped nuts (walnuts or almonds)

Stir jello in water until it is dissolved. Add a can of jellied cranberry sauce and break up with fork. Stir until cranberry is almost melted. Add salt. Refrigerate until partially firm then gently fold in sour cream and chopped nuts. Pour into a serving dish, chill and serve.

Classic French Vinaigrette Dressing

  1/4   c white wine vinegar
    2   T Dijon mustard
    1   T tarragon, crushed
    1   c olive oil
        Fresh ground pepper
        Salt, to taste

Combine all ingredients in a blender. Serve chilled on a green leaf lettuce salad.

Cranberry Mold

    1 8oz can crushed pineapple, drained (reserve syrup)
    2 3oz pkgs lemon-flavored gelatin
 1/2 c sugar
    1 c peeled and diced apples
    1 lb raw cranberries, ground or very finely chopped
 1/2 c finely chopped almonds, pecans or walnuts

Add water to pineapple syrup to make 3 cups. Heat until boiling; add lemon-flavored gelatin and sugar. Stir until thoroughly dissolved. Cool and chill. When mixture is slightly thickened, add pineapple, apples, cranberries and nuts. Pour into a 9"x13" pan. Chill until firm.

Cream of Broccoli Caliente

    2 c chicken broth
    1 c broccoli, chopped
    2 T butter
    1 med yellow onion, chopped
    1 med jalapeno, minced
    1 c whipping cream
    2 egg yolks
 1-2 t crushed red pepper flakes

Simmer broccoli in the broth while browning the onion in butter in separate saucepan. Add onion to the simmering broccoli. Cover and continue to simmer for 25 minutes. Pour broccoli and broth into blender and puree. Return to sauce pan, add jalapeno and cook on low heat. In separate bowl, beat cream and egg yolks until just blended. Slowly stir into soup. Continue heating for 4 or 5 minutes. Serve. Sprinkle with crushed pepper flakes. Delicious with cornbread.

Crunchy Pea Salad

Salad: 1 10oz pkg frozen baby peas
         1 c celery, diced
         1 c cauliflower, chopped
         1 c green onion, diced
         1 c cashews, chopped
         8 lg lettuce leaves

Sour Cream Dressing:
         1/2 c sour cream
         1   c prepared ranch style dressing

Garnish: 4 slices bacon, cooked and crumbled

Thaw package of peas. Gently toss salad ingredients together, except lettuce and bacon. Combine dressing ingredients; drizzle over salad. Chill for about 2 hours.

Place chilled salad on lettuce leaves and garnish with crumbled bacon slices.

Serves 4-6

Cucumber Papaya Salad

         1 lg cucumber, peeled, seeded and thinly sliced
               (about 1 1/2 cups)
       1/2 t salt
       1/4 c rice wine vinegar
         4 t sugar
         1 t peanut oil
            Hawaiian chilies, minced or chili paste, to taste
         2 t fresh ginger, minced
         1 lg papaya, peeled and diced (about 1 1/2 cups)
       1/4 c fresh cilantro, chopped
         6 lg lettuce leaves

Sprinkle cucumber with salt and let drain in a colander for 20 minutes. Rinse and pat dry. In a bowl, whisk together vinegar, sugar, oil, chilies, and ginger. Add cucumber, papaya, and cilantro. Toss and serve on lettuce leaves.

Serves 4-6

Dried Cranberry and Wild Rice Salad

1/3 c wild rice (cooked according to the package directions)
2/3 c long grain rice
3/4 c pecans, toasted and coarsely chopped
3/4 c dried cranberries
1/3 c celery, finely chopped
1/4 c scallions, thinly sliced
3 T extra virgin olive oil
2 T balsamic vinegar
1/2 t salt
1/2 t freshly ground pepper

Cook long grain rice and wild rice separately according to individual instructions. Let cool completely. About an hour before serving, mix together rice, pecans, cranberries, celery and scallions and toss until mixed. In a small bowl, whisk together oil, vinegar, salt and pepper. Pour over rice mixture.

Serves 6

Egg Drop Soup

2 qt rich chicken stock
6 eggs, beaten
1/2 t white pepper
1 t sesame oil
1/4 c Chinese parsley, chopped

Bring chicken stock to a full boil in a stockpot. In separate bowl, beat together eggs, white pepper and sesame oil. Remove stockpot from heat. Slowly add egg mixture in a steady stream. Let eggs go to bottom of broth, then float back up to the top. Eggs will be in the shape of flowers and be very light and delicate in texture. Stir in Chinese parsley and serve at once.

Fourth of July Potato Salad

 2   lbs red potatoes, cooked and cut in 1/2-inch cubes
1/2 c green bell pepper, chopped
1/4 c radishes or green onions, thinly sliced
 2   T fresh parsley, minced
 1   c celery, chopped

Dressing:
1/4 c cider vinegar
 2   T vegetable oil
 2   T Dijon mustard
1/2 t salt
1/4 t freshly ground pepper
1/4 t celery seed

In a blender, combine dressing ingredients and blend until smooth. Refrigerate for at least one hour before serving. Combine potatoes, green peppers, radishes or green onions, parsley and celery. Pour dressing over salad and toss gently.

French Onion Soup

 2   onions, thinly sliced
 2   cloves garlic, minced
 4   T butter
 4   T flour
 2   10 3/4oz cans chicken broth
     Water
 4   French bread slices, toasted
 1   c Swiss cheese, grated

Preheat oven to 400°.

Sauté onions and garlic in butter until golden. Sprinkle with flour and stir until browned and bubbly. Add chicken broth and 2 cans of water. Simmer 20-30 minutes. Pour into ovenproof bowls. Top with toasted French bread slices and grated Swiss cheese. Place in oven for 5 minutes, or until cheese is golden and bubbly.

Serves 8

Fruit Salad Delight

1 3/4oz pkg regular (not instant) vanilla pudding mix
3/4 c pineapple juice

Mix juice and pudding mix in small saucepan. Cook on stove until thick. Cool.

Add:
1 lg can pineapple chunks, drained
1 lg can mandarin oranges, drained
1 lg jar cherries, drained

Refrigerate.

Next morning or later add:
3 bananas (sliced)
1 handful chopped pecans
1 handful white raisins

Mix and serve.

Makes 2 cups

Green Goddess Dressing

1 c mayonnaise
1 clove garlic, minced
3 anchovy fillets, minced
1/4 c chives or green onions, finely minced
1/4 c parsley, minced
1 T lemon juice
1 T tarragon vinegar
1/2 t salt
1/2 t ground pepper
1/2 c sour cream

Combine all ingredients and blend well.

Layered Tuna Tofu Salad

Salad: 1 block firm tofu, drained and cubed
             1 can tuna, drained
             1 med Kula onion, sliced
          2-3 tomatoes, cubed

Dressing:
          1/3 c mild shoyu
          1/3 c sugar
          1/3 c rice vinegar

Garnish: 3 T parsley, chopped
           1 green onion, chopped

    Layer salad ingredients in a glass bowl. Do not toss. Mix dressing ingredients in a bottle. Shake well. Pour over salad before serving. Garnish with parsley and green onion.

Lentil Soup

1 c lentils, washed and drained
1 c split peas, washed and drained
Cold water
1 T butter
2 T oil
3 cloves garlic, finely chopped
2 sm onions, chopped
1 lg rib of celery and leaves, chopped
2 carrots, thickly sliced
2 T parsley, chopped
Freshly ground black pepper
1/4-1/2 c miso paste

Place lentils and split peas in a large bowl and cover with cold water. Let soak while preparing other vegetables. Heat butter and oil in heavy kettle. Add garlic, onions, celery, carrots and parsley. Sauté for 5 minutes over medium heat. When onions have wilted, drain lentils and split peas and add to the kettle. Add pepper and 1 1/2 quarts of cold fresh water; bring to boil. Lower heat, cover and simmer until vegetables are tender, about 1 1/2 hours. Remove 1/2 c of the broth, mix with miso paste until smooth and return to kettle. Cook 20 minutes longer and serve.

Mushroom Barley Soup

Serves 6-8

3 c mushroom slices (about 1/2 lb)
1/2 c round onion, chopped
1/2 c green pepper, chopped
1/3 c butter or margarine
1/3 c flour
3 c water
2 c milk
1/2 c quick barley
2 t Worcestershire sauce
1 1/2 t salt

continued...

1 t dried parsley flakes
Dash of pepper

Sauté mushrooms, onion and green pepper in butter. Blend in flour; continue cooking over medium heat until flour is browned. Gradually add water and milk; add remaining ingredients. Bring to boil, stirring frequently; reduce heat. Cover and simmer 10-20 minutes or until barley is tender, stirring occasionally.

Serves 6-8

Orange Avocado Salad

2 heads romaine lettuce, chopped
1 c celery, chopped
2 green onions and stems, chopped
1/4 c toasted slivered almonds
1 orange, peeled and cubed
1 avocado, peeled and cubed

Dressing:
1/2 t salt
Dash ground pepper
1/4 t Tabasco sauce
2 T sugar
2 T balsamic vinegar
1/4 c salad oil

Combine salad ingredients in large bowl. In separate bowl, mix dressing ingredients. Pour over salad and toss.

Overnight Layered Salad

    1 head iceberg lettuce, shredded
  1/2 c green onion, sliced
    1 c celery, thinly sliced
    1 8oz can water chestnuts, drained and sliced
    1 10oz pkg frozen peas
    2 c mayonnaise
    2 tsp sugar
  1/2 c parmesan cheese, grated
    1 tsp garlic powder
  1/2 lb bacon, cooked crisp
    3 hard boiled eggs, chopped
    2 med tomatoes, cut into wedges

In a shallow glass serving bowl, place layer of lettuce. Top with a layer each of onion, celery, water chestnuts and frozen peas. Spread evenly with mayonnaise. Sprinkle with sugar, cheese and garlic powder. Cover and refrigerate overnight (or at least several hours).

Before serving, crumble bacon on top, sprinkle with chopped eggs and arrange tomato wedges.

Pasta Tortellini Salad

    2 pkgs cheese tortellini
  1/2 c Chinese snow peas or snap peas, trimmed
    2 lg tomatoes, chopped

Vinaigrette:
    1 c olive oil
    6 T white vinegar
    2 t basil and/or dill
    4 T green onion, minced
    2 garlic cloves
    1 t sugar

      Fresh ground pepper

      continued...

Garnish:
    1/2 c parmesan cheese, shredded

Vinaigrette:
    Whisk together all of the above ingredients into a small bowl or measuring cup and set overnight.

Salad:
    Cook cheese tortellini according to package directions. Two minutes before done, add peas. Drain and rinse with cold water. Add tomatoes. Toss with vinaigrette and pepper. Garnish with parmesan cheese before serving.

Makes 3/4 cup

Poppy Seed Salad Dressing

    3 T cider vinegar
    3 T sugar
  1/2 t dry mustard
  1/2 t salt
    6 T oil
    1 t poppy seeds

    Mix all ingredients together in a shaker bottle or cruet. Refrigerate until chilled.

    This is a favorite dressing for a citrus salad with butter lettuce, mandarin oranges or strawberries sliced, red onion sliced thin and toasted almonds.

Portuguese Bean Soup

      6 oz dry red kidney beans (soak overnight in water)
      1 T oil
      2 6oz sticks Portuguese sausage
    1/2 c carrots, diced large
      1 c onions, diced large
    3/4 c celery, diced large
    1/2 c bell pepper, diced large
      1 T garlic, chopped
      1 t ginger, chopped
      1 bay leaf
      1 t paprika
    1/8 t marjoram
    1/8 t basil
      2 qts beef or chicken stock
      2 c cabbage, diced large
      1 c potatoes, diced
      1 smoked ham hock
      1 can diced tomato or 2 c fresh tomatoes
         Salt and pepper to taste

Clean and soak beans overnight. In a large pot over low flame, heat oil. Sauté the sausage until fat is rendered. Increase heat and add the diced vegetables (except cabbage and tomato) and sauté till transparent (5 minutes). Add garlic, ginger and herbs.

Stir and sauté for 2 minutes. Add stock and ham hock and bring to a boil. Lower heat and simmer for one hour (adding the beans and potatoes about half hour after lowering heat). When beans are soft, add cabbage and tomatoes. Continue to cook. Remove ham hock and dice. Return to soup and season with salt and pepper. Thicken slightly if desired.

Refreshing Gazpacho

        2   lg tomatoes, coarsely chopped
        1   med cucumber, coarsely chopped
        1   med green pepper, coarsely chopped
        1   clove garlic, coarsely chopped
        2   green onions, coarsely chopped
        2   sprigs fresh parsley
        1   T fresh basil or 1 t dried basil
    1 1/2   c tomato juice
        1   T wine vinegar
        1   T olive oil
      2-4   T lemon juice
             Hot sauce to taste
             Salt and pepper to taste
             Shoyu to taste

Garnish: Croutons and parmesan cheese

Combine all ingredients. Blend in blender until desired texture (about 2 cups at a time). Chill and serve with croutons and parmesan cheese.

Saffron Rice Salad

        2   pkgs Saffron Rice, prepared according to directions
        2   sm cans sliced black olives, drained
        1   c cooked frozen peas
      1/2   c slivered almonds, toasted
      1/2   red bell pepper, diced
      1/2   green bell pepper, diced
        1   can garbanzo beans, drained
        1   tomato, diced
        3   T red wine vinegar
        3   T olive oil
             Salt and pepper

Mix oil, vinegar, salt and pepper, in bottom of serving bowl. Add rice and all other ingredients. Mix well and serve.

Shrimp and Pasta Salad Delight

    2 c shell macaroni, cooked and drained.
    1 c celery, chopped
    1/2 c onion, chopped
    1/2 c green pepper, chopped
    2 7oz pkgs frozen cooked shrimp (thawed) or
        2 large cans of small to medium shrimp

Place cooked macaroni in large bowl. Add above ingredients and mix well.

Dressing: 1 c mayonnaise
           1 c brown sugar
           1 T vinegar
           1 t salt

Garnish:
           1/2 c cashews, chopped

Combine dressing ingredients. Toss with pasta and shrimp mixture. Garnish with cashews and serve.

Spinach Salad

Salad: 1 lb fresh spinach
           1 9oz can sliced water chestnuts, drained
           1/4 lb mushrooms, sliced
           1 sm red onion, thinly sliced

Dressing:
           1/3 c vegetable oil
           1/4 c sugar
           1/4 c chili sauce
           2 T red wine vinegar
           1/2 t Worcestershire sauce

           continued...

    1   sm onion, finely chopped
  1/2   t dry mustard
  1/2   t salt
  1/4   t cayenne pepper

Garnish: 2   hard boiled eggs, grated
        3/4   c bacon, cooked and crumbled

Mix salad ingredients in a large bowl and set aside. Mix dressing ingredients together in small bowl. Just before serving pour dressing over salad, toss and sprinkle with egg and bacon.

Serves 6

Super Easy Chicken Gumbo

    2   T bacon or chicken fat
    1   med onion, diced
  1/3   c green pepper, diced
    1   qt chicken broth
    1   16oz can tomatoes, undrained
    2   t salt
  1/8   t pepper
  1/3   c uncooked rice
    2   T parsley, chopped
    1   bay leaf
    1   lb sausage (cut up and cooked)
  2-3   c chicken, cooked and cubed
    1   c okra, frozen or canned, cut-up

Put all ingredients except sausage, chicken and okra in pot. Cover and simmer for 40 minutes. Add sausage, chicken and okra and continue to simmer another 20 minutes. Remove bay leaf and serve.

Top Ramen Cabbage Salad

Serves 6-8

Dressing:

    1/2 c oil
    1/4 c wine vinegar
    1/4 c sugar
      1 t pepper
      1 pkg Top Ramen seasoning packet (any flavor)

Salad: 1 pkg, Top Ramen noodles, uncooked, broken into pieces
          1 med head cabbage, coarsely chopped
          1 c almond slivers, toasted

Combine dressing ingredients. Mix well.
Toss with cabbage, ramen, and almonds. Serve immediately.

Optional: Add cooked chicken pieces for a salad meal.

Very Ono Salad Dressing

Makes about 2 cups

      1 c salad oil
    3/4 c sugar
    1/3 c white vinegar
    1/2 t salt
    1/2 t pepper
    1/2 t prepared mustard
    1/2 t Worcestershire sauce
         Few slices round onion
      2 cloves garlic
      2 bay leaves

Blend all ingredients in blender on high speed for 5 minutes.

Waipahu French Dressing

1 1/2 c vegetable oil
    3 t white vinegar
  1/3 c mayonnaise
    1 c catsup
    1 t prepared mustard
  1/2 c sugar
    1 t Worcestershire sauce
    2 t salt
    1 t soy sauce
    1 t black pepper

Combine all ingredients in a blender, until smooth and creamy. Pour into a jar and chill. Keeps for 1-2 months refrigerated.

Vegetables
&
Side Dishes

Vegetables & Side Dishes

Artichoke Pie

- 2 jars of artichoke hearts, chopped (reserve liquid of one jar)
- 2 med onions, chopped
- 1/2 lb mushrooms, sliced
- 5 eggs, lightly beaten
- 1 box frozen chopped spinach, thawed and well-drained
- 2/3 c cheddar cheese, grated
- Salt and pepper to taste

Preheat oven to 350°. Sauté onions and mushrooms in oil of one jar of artichoke hearts. Add to eggs. Add artichokes, spinach, cheese, salt and pepper. Mix well. Bake in greased 9" pie plate for 45 minutes or until set.

Broccoli Cream Linguine

Serves 8

- 1/2 lb fresh broccoli, cut into florets
- 1/2 lb linguine
- 2 c half and half cream
- 1/2 lb fresh mushrooms, sliced
- 1/2 clove garlic, minced
- 1/4 c butter
- 1 c parmesan cheese, grated

Boil broccoli 5-7 minutes until tender. Remove with a slotted spoon and set aside. Using broccoli water, boil linguine until done. Drain. Combine broccoli, linguine, and cream.

Sauté mushrooms and garlic in butter for 4-5 minutes. Add mushroom mixture to broccoli and pasta mixture. Toss in cheese and serve.

Broiled Tomato Duxelles

      2   med tomatoes
     12   med mushrooms, finely chopped
      2   sm sweet onions, finely chopped
      4   T butter
    1/4   c dry sherry
      1   t fresh lemon juice
    1/4   t salt
           Dash of pepper
      1   egg yolk
      1   T parmesan cheese, grated

Preheat oven to 350°. Slice tomatoes in half. Place the 4 halves in a buttered pie plate. In saucepan, sauté mushrooms and onions in butter for one minute. Add sherry, lemon juice, salt and pepper. Simmer 5-10 minutes until liquid is absorbed. Remove pan from heat and stir in egg yolk. Spread mixture over tomato halves. Sprinkle halves with parmesan cheese. Bake for 10 minutes. Place under broiler for a minute or so, until tops are brown.

Favorite Quiche

      1 frozen deep-dish pie crust
     12 slices bacon, crisp and crumbled
      1 c swiss cheese, shredded
    1/3 c onion, finely chopped
      4 eggs
      2 c half and half cream
    3/4 t salt
    1/4 t black pepper
    1/8 t cayenne

Preheat oven to 425°. Remove frozen pie crust from freezer and thaw for 5 minutes. Sprinkle bacon, cheese and onion on bottom of pie crust. In a large bowl, beat eggs slightly; blend in remaining ingredients. Pour egg mixture carefully over bacon, cheese and onion. Bake uncovered for 15 minutes.

Reduce oven temperature to 300° Bake uncovered until knife inserted halfway between center and edge comes out clean, about 30 minutes. Let stand 10 minutes before cutting.

Four Cheese Quiche with Red Pepper

    9" or 10" pie crust, prebaked for 5 minutes at 375°.

      4 oz blue cheese, crumbled
      3 oz swiss cheese, grated
      4 oz brie cheese, broken in small bits
  1 1/2 c heavy cream
      3 eggs
    1/8 t nutmeg
         Salt and pepper to taste
    1/4 c cream cheese
   1 lg red bell pepper
      2 T butter, melted

      continued...

Preheat oven to 375°.

Mix swiss and brie cheeses together and set aside. In blender or food processor, blend well cream, eggs, nutmeg, salt and pepper and cream cheese. Slice bell peppers into rounds, removing seeds and membrane and sauté in butter until soft. Remove from heat.

Sprinkle swiss and brie mixture on crust. Top with sautéed pepper rings. Pour custard over peppers. Bake 10 minutes. Reduce heat to 350° and bake for 20-25 minutes longer or until inserted knife comes out clean.

Serves 8-10

Gon Lo Mein (Chinese noodles)

1/2 lb char siu (cooked sweet red pork), thinly sliced
1 lb E-min noodles
1 med onion, thinly sliced
1 pkg bean sprouts or chop suey mix
1 stalk celery, thinly sliced
1 t salt
3 T oyster sauce
2 T shoyu
1 T sesame seeds
1 T sesame oil
2 T oil
Parsley or cilantro for garnish

Preheat oven to 350°. Combine all of the ingredients. Place in a 9"x13" baking pan. Bake for 15 minutes. Garnish noodles with sprigs of fresh parsley or cilantro.

Green Rice

1 c cooked rice
1 1/2 c sharp cheese, grated
1 c milk
1 egg, slightly beaten
1/2 med onion, chopped
1/2 t salt
1 10oz box frozen spinach, thawed and well-drained
1/4 c butter, melted

Preheat oven to 350°. Combine ingredients and pour into greased 1 1/2 quart casserole dish. Cover. Bake 40 minutes.

Gulliver's Corn

2 pkgs frozen corn, thawed
1 c whipping cream
1 t salt
1 t sugar
2 T butter
2 t flour
Grated parmesan cheese

Drain corn and cook in cream to boil; reduce heat, simmer 5 minutes. Stir in salt, sugar and butter. Stir in flour and continue simmering until slightly thick. Pour into 2 quart casserole dish, sprinkle with cheese, dot with butter. Broil until golden brown.

Jalapeño Potatoes

8 med boiling potatoes (about 4 lbs)
  Salt and pepper to taste
1 green bell pepper, chopped
8 green onions, chopped
1 c butter, melted
2 T flour
2 c milk
1 roll (6oz) jalapeño cheese
1 roll (6oz) garlic cheese
1 jar (4oz) pimientos, drained

Preheat oven to 350°. Boil potatoes until just tender. Peel and slice. In a flat buttered 3-quart casserole, layer potato slices and season with salt and pepper. Sauté bell peppers and onions in 1/2 cup butter until tender. Set aside. In saucepan, combine flour and 1/2 cup butter and stir until bubbly. Add milk and cheeses and stir over medium heat until cheese melts. Add onion mixture and pimientos. Blend well. Pour over potatoes and bake for 45 minutes. This is best when assembled the day before.

Maple-Glazed Sweet Potatoes and Apples

3 lbs orange-fleshed sweet potatoes, peeled,
cut crosswise into 1/4 inch rounds
1 3/4 lbs tart green apples, peeled, halved, cored,
cut into 1/4-inch-thick slices
3/4 c pure maple syrup
1/4 c apple cider
1/4 c (1/2 stick) unsalted butter, cut into pieces
1/2 t salt

Preheat oven to 375°. In 9"x13" glass baking dish, alternate potato and apple slices in rows, packing tightly. (Stand the slices on end.) Combine remaining ingredients in heavy medium saucepan and bring to boil over high heat. Pour hot syrup over potatoes and apples. Cover dish tightly with foil and bake 35 minutes. Uncover casserole. (Can do this up to 3 hours ahead. Let stand at room temperature, basting occasionally with pan juices.) Reduce temperature to 350°. Bake for 30 minutes until potatoes and apples are very tender. Baste occasionally. Syrup will be reduced to thick glaze. Let stand 10 minutes before serving.

Night Before Mashed Potatoes

8-10 potatoes, peeled
8 oz cream cheese, softened
1 c sour cream
Salt and pepper to taste
Butter
Seasoned salt
3 cloves garlic, crushed

Boil and drain potatoes. Whip hot potatoes, adding cream cheese and sour cream. Continue beating until fluffy and smooth. Add salt and pepper. Place in a buttered 9"x13" baking dish. Dot generously with butter and sprinkle with seasoned salt. Cover with foil and refrigerate overnight. (Potatoes can be frozen at this stage and thawed before baking). Bake, covered with foil, 15 minutes at 325°. Uncover and continue baking for 20 minutes.

Potato Gratinée

- 1/4 c melted butter and olive oil, mixed
- 1 t fresh thyme leaves (1/4 teaspoon dried)
- 2 lbs baking potatoes, thinly sliced
  - Salt
  - Freshly ground pepper
- 8oz Fontina cheese, grated
- 1/2 c heavy cream
- 3/4 c whole-wheat bread crumbs tossed
  with 1/3 cup melted butter

Preheat oven to 350°. Coat the bottom of a large casserole dish with a tablespoon or so of the butter/olive oil mixture. Cover the bottom of the pan with 1 layer of overlapping potato slices. Season with salt, pepper, thyme and some of the cheese. Continue this layering process, finishing with a layer of potatoes. Drizzle the remaining butter and oil mixture and the cream slowly over top. Cover pan with aluminum foil and bake until potatoes are tender, about 45 minutes. Remove foil, top with bread crumb mixture and broil until top is brown and crisp.

Rosemary Potato Crisps

Serves 4-6

- 12 sm unpeeled red potatoes, thinly sliced
- 4 T olive oil
- 2 t fresh rosemary, chopped
- 1 t salt
- 6 turns freshly ground black pepper

Preheat oven to 400°. Toss potato slices in a bowl with the oil, rosemary, salt, and pepper. Spread on a baking sheet in a single layer and bake for 15 to 20 minutes. Remove from the oven and turn with a spatula. Bake until golden brown and crisp, about 35 minutes. Remove from oven and serve immediately.

Southern Style Rice Perlo

          12   oz lean bacon, diced
           1   lg onion, diced
         1/2   t black pepper
           1   15oz can crushed tomatoes
         1/2   c water
         1/2   c sugar
           3   c long grain rice (Uncle Ben's is best for this dish)

In a 4 quart (or larger) pan, sauté bacon, covered, on medium heat for 10 minutes. Add diced onion, cover and sauté another 10 minutes. Add pepper, tomatoes, water and sugar and stir well. Stir in rice. Cover pot and cook on low heat for approximately 25 minutes. Stir well again, cover and cook on low heat for an additional 15 minutes, stirring frequently so the rice does not stick together and until liquid is mostly absorbed. (Especially good as a side dish with pork, but can be used with beef or other meats.)

Note: Always use a fork while stirring this recipe, to keep the rice loose.

Spanish Rice

           1   lb ground beef
         1/4   c onion, chopped
         1-2   cloves garlic, minced
         1/4   c bell pepper, chopped
           1   c uncooked rice
           1   14 1/2oz can stewed tomatoes
           2   8oz cans tomato sauce
           1   t cumin
         1/2   t oregano
       1/2-1   T chili powder
               Salt and pepper to taste
         1/2   c cheddar cheese, grated

               continued...

Brown meat in large saucepan. Drain and set aside. Sauté onion, garlic and bell pepper. Add meat to onion mixture. Stir in all other ingredients except cheese. Cover and bring to a boil. Reduce heat and simmer 30-40 minutes. Let stand 10 minutes. Top with grated cheddar and serve.

Stuffed Zucchini

3 med zucchini
2 T butter
1 c fresh mushrooms, chopped
2 T flour
1/4 t dried oregano, crushed
1 c monterey jack cheese, shredded
2 T pimiento, chopped (optional)
1/4 c parmesan cheese, grated

Cook whole zucchini in boiling salted water about 10 minutes or until tender. Drain. Cut in half lengthwise. Scoop out centers (save), leaving a 1/4 inch thick shell. Chop center portion and set aside.

Melt butter in a large skillet; sauté mushrooms until tender. Stir in flour and oregano; remove from heat. Stir in Monterey Jack cheese and pimiento; stir in the reserved chopped zucchini. Heat mixture through.

Preheat broiler. Fill zucchini shells, using about 1/4 cup filling for each. Sprinkle with parmesan cheese. Broil several inches from source of heat until hot and bubbly.

Note: May be assembled in advance, covered and refrigerated up to 4 hours.

Three Cheese Quiche

1	9" prepared pie shell, unbaked (recipe follows)
1	c swiss cheese, grated
1/2	c marbled jack cheese, grated
3	T romano cheese, grated
1/2	c med onion, chopped
1	c fresh broccoli florets, chopped
1/2	c fresh mushrooms, sliced
1/4	t dried marjoram
1/2	t dried basil
1/4	t salt
1/2	t garlic powder
3	eggs
1	c milk
1/2	c half and half
7-8	cherry tomatoes
1	T romano cheese, grated

Preheat oven to 425°. Sprinkle cheeses over the bottom of pie shell, then evenly distribute onion, broccoli and mushrooms over cheese layer. Mix eggs and spices together in a bowl. Add milk and half and half. Mix well. Pour over contents in pie shell.

Cut cherry tomatoes in halves and place, cut side up, in a ring on top of mixture. Sprinkle the romano over the top. Bake for 15 minutes. Turn oven down to 300° and bake an additional 45-55 minutes or until knife inserted in middle comes out clean.

Pie Crust:
1	c flour
1	T butter-flavored shortening
1/2	t salt
1/4	t sugar
3	T cold water

Blend first four ingredients together with pastry blender until crumbly (like coarse cornmeal). Add cold water, 1 tablespoon at a time, mixing with a fork until mixture holds well together. Handle as little as possible. Shape into a patty and wrap in plastic wrap. Chill for at least 1 hour. Roll out between saran wrap with very little flour. Place carefully in a pie plate, being careful not to stretch dough. Trim edges.

Notes

Entrées

Entrées

Baked Chicken Dijon

3 T fresh parsley, minced
5 T parmesan cheese, freshly grated
1 1/2 c panko flakes
1 clove garlic, crushed
1/2 c butter or margarine
6 T Dijon mustard
4 boneless chicken breasts, skinned

Garnish: Freshly grated parmesan cheese

Combine parsley, parmesan cheese and panko flakes; set aside. Sauté garlic in butter until lightly browned. Stir in mustard. Remove from heat and cool slightly. Whip vigorously until mixture thickens. Dip chicken in mustard marinade until well coated. Then dip into parmesan mixture, packing crumbs onto chicken. Place breaded chicken into a lightly greased baking dish. Repeat for each chicken breast. Cover and refrigerate for several hours to set crumbs. Preheat oven to 350°. Bake uncovered for 20 minutes, or until chicken is lightly browned. Top with grated parmesan cheese.

Chicken and Vegetable Stir Fry

2 T soy sauce
1 1/2 T rice wine or dry sherry
2 t cornstarch
1 lb boneless chicken, cut into 1/2-inch cubes
1 T vegetable oil
2 t fresh ginger, chopped
2 t garlic, minced
1/2 c carrots, diced
1 sm Maui onion, diced
1/2 c celery, diced
1/2 c zucchini, diced
1 c chicken broth
4 t shoyu
2 t sesame oil
1 t sugar
Cornstarch for thickening
Cashews (optional)

Combine the first three ingredients and mix in the chicken. Marinate in refrigerator for 30 minutes. Place a wok over high heat, add oil and quickly stir fry chicken. When chicken is cooked, remove from wok and set aside. Add ginger and garlic to wok. Cook for five seconds, then add the carrots and cook for two minutes. Add onion, celery, zucchini and broth. Combine soy sauce, sesame oil and sugar and add to the vegetables. Use cornstarch to thicken sauce; cook until sauce thickens. Add in cooked chicken. Stir in cashews just before serving with rice.

Chicken Taco Casserole

- 1   can cream of mushroom soup
- 1   can cream of chicken soup
- 1/2   c salsa
- 1/2   soup can milk
- 1/2   onion, chopped
- 1   can black olives, sliced
-    Bell pepper, chopped
-    Mushrooms, sliced
- 1   can corn
- 1   pkg corn tortillas (sliced into strips)
-    Cheddar cheese, grated
-    Chicken, cooked and cubed

Preheat oven to 350°. In a large bowl mix together soups, salsa, milk, onion, olives, pepper, mushrooms and corn. Pour 1/2 c sauce on bottom of 9"x13" baking pan and begin layering: sauce, tortillas, chicken, and cheese. Repeat, ending with cheese. Cover and bake for 30-40 minutes, until bubbly.

Chicken Tetrazzini

- 1   8oz pkg spaghetti noodles
- 1/2   c celery, diced
- 1/2   c onion, diced
- 1/2   c bell pepper, diced
- 1/4   c butter or margarine
- 1-2   lbs cooked chicken, skinned, boned and diced
- 1   sm jar pimientos, drained
- 1-2   T chili peppers, chopped (optional)
- 1/2   lb sharp cheddar cheese, grated
- 1   4oz can mushrooms, drained
- 1   can cream of mushroom soup
- 1   can chicken broth
-    Salt and pepper to taste
-    Parmesan cheese

continued...

Boil spaghetti noodles; rinse with cool water and drain. Sauté vegetables in butter until cooked but firm.

Preheat oven to 350°.

Combine noodles with sautéed vegetables and chicken. Add pimientos and remaining ingredients, except parmesan cheese. Pour mixture into a casserole dish and top with parmesan cheese. Bake for approximately 1 hour.

Chicken Wild Rice

1	10 1/2oz can cream of celery soup
1	10 1/2oz can cream of mushroom soup
2 1/2	cans water
1	c long grain rice
1	pkg long grain and wild rice (example: Uncle Ben's)
2	lbs boneless, skinless chicken thighs/breast
1/2	lb margarine, melted
1/2	c almond slivers

Preheat oven to 325°. Mix both types of soup together and add water. Place two types of rice mixture in 9"x13" buttered pan. Pour soup/water mixture over rice. Dip cut-up chicken in melted margarine. Place on top of rice mixture. Sprinkle seasonings from Uncle Ben's package. Cover with foil and bake in oven for one hour. Uncover, sprinkle with almond slivers and bake for 30 minutes or more.

Country Chicken Pie

1 sm onion, chopped
1 c celery, thinly sliced
1 c carrots, thinly sliced
1 c mushrooms, sliced
3 c cooked chicken (or turkey) cubed
1 T flour
1 10 3/4oz can cream of mushroom soup
   (98% fat free can be substituted)
1 c frozen peas (cooked)
   Dash of pepper

1 pkg ready-made pie crusts (for 2 pies)

Preheat oven to 350°. Sauté onions, celery and carrots in a little margarine or butter flavored spray until tender (5 minutes); add mushrooms and sauté 2 more minutes. Toss chicken or turkey cubes with flour in large bowl. Stir in soup, sautéed vegetables, and cooked peas. Add pepper and mix. Prepare pie crust according to package directions. Use one for bottom of deep-dish 9" pie pan. Fill shell with turkey mixture. Second pie crust should be cut into 1/2"strips. Weave strips (lattice effect) over top of pie and crimp edges.

Bake for 40 minutes.

French Chicken In Orange Sherry Sauce

3 lg chicken breasts, split (about 2 1/2 lbs)
1/2 t salt
1 c mushrooms, sliced
1 onion, sliced
1/2 c bell pepper, chopped

Sauce: 1 c orange juice
1/4 c sherry
1/2 c water
1 T brown sugar, firmly packed
1 t salt
1/4 t pepper
1 t grated orange peel
1 T flour
2 t parsley, chopped

Garnish: Paprika
1 orange, peeled and sliced

Brown chicken in broiler skin side up. Place in shallow baking dish. Sprinkle with salt and pepper.
Preheat oven to 375°.
Add mushrooms, onion and bell pepper; set aside.
Combine all of the sauce ingredients in a saucepan. Cook until thickened. Pour over chicken and bake 15 minutes. Baste several times. Garnish with paprika and orange slices before serving.

Hawaiian Sweet and Sour Chicken

        1/4 c butter
      2 1/4 lbs chicken thighs
          1 8oz can pineapple chunks, reserve juice
          1 t salt
        1/4 c brown sugar
          2 T cornstarch
          2 T chili sauce
          1 t shoyu
        1/4 c vinegar
        1/2 t Worcestershire sauce
        1/3 c catsup

Preheat oven to 350°.
Melt butter and pour into shallow roasting pan. Roll chicken in butter until well coated and lay in a single layer, skin side up.
Combine reserved pineapple juice and remaining ingredients in a saucepan and simmer, stirring constantly until mixture thickens. Add pineapple chunks and spoon 1/2 of the sauce over the chicken. Bake for 1 hour and 15 minutes, basting occasionally with remaining sauce.

Italian Chicken

          3 lbs boneless chicken breasts
             Flour
          2 6oz jars marinated artichoke hearts
          4 T olive oil
          2 cans whole tomatoes, drained
          4 cloves garlic, minced
          1 lb mushrooms, sliced
          1 c sherry
      1 1/2 t salt
        3/4 t pepper
          1 t oregano
          2 t basil

             continued...

Preheat oven to 350°. Cut chicken into bite-sized chunks and dust with flour. Drain artichoke hearts, reserving the liquid. Brown the chicken in the liquid and olive oil. Place the browned chicken in a casserole.

Combine remaining ingredients, except drained artichokes, and pour over chicken. Bake for 50 minutes, uncovered. Remove from oven, add artichokes and continue baking 10 minutes longer.

Kung Pao Chicken

Marinade: 1 T soy sauce
1 t sugar
1/2 t salt
1/2 t cornstarch dissolved in 1 T water
1 t oil
1 lb chicken, boned and diced

Mix together and toss with chicken. Marinate for 20 minutes.

Sauce: 1 c chicken stock or chicken bouillon
1 T soy sauce
1 T vinegar
1 t sugar
1 t salt
1 t cornstarch dissolved in 1 T hot water

Combine thoroughly and set aside.

3-4 T peanut oil
2 t fresh ginger, crushed
2 t garlic, crushed
7 Chinese green onions, bottoms only, cut into 1" pieces
10 peppercorns
10 pods dried red chilies, cut into small pieces

Garnish: Unsalted peanuts, chopped

Heat oil in wok or heavy skillet. Sauté chicken until tender. Remove chicken and clean wok. Add ginger, garlic, green onions, peppercorns and chilies to wok and cook 1 minute. Add chicken and toss for 1-2 minutes. Pour sauce over chicken and cook until thickened. Top with peanuts.

Mushroom Chicken Casserole

- 6 boneless, skinless chicken breasts or equivalent in Breast Tenders (enough to cover the bottom of the pan)
- Salt, pepper, and paprika
- 1/4 c butter, melted
- 1/4 c cooking sherry
- 2 cans cream of mushroom soup
- 1 sm can mushrooms, sliced
- 1/4 t basil
- 1/2 c onion, chopped
- 2/3 c lemon juice

Preheat oven to 350°. Place chicken in a 9"x13" baking dish. Sprinkle with salt, pepper, and paprika. Mix remaining ingredients and pour over chicken. Cook for 1 hour and 15 minutes.
Serve over rice or noodles.

Oyster Sauce Chicken on Noodles

Serves 6-8

- 2 lbs chicken breast
- 1 T soy sauce
- 1/4 c flour
- 2 pkgs chow mein noodles
- 1 T salad oil
- 2 cloves garlic, minced
- 2 c broccoli
- 1/2 c oyster sauce
- 1 T sugar
- 1 can chicken broth
- 1 T cornstarch
- 1 t water

Preheat oven to 250°. Cut chicken into pieces and mix with soy sauce. Coat chicken with flour. Heat noodles in oven for 10 minutes. In wok, brown garlic in oil and discard garlic. Fry chicken in wok and remove. Stir fry broccoli, then add chicken, oyster sauce, sugar and broth. Mix cornstarch with water and add to mixture. Serve over noodles.

Shoyu Chicken

3/4 c shoyu
2 T honey
1/2 c brown sugar
2 T ginger powder
1/2 c green onions, chopped
1 1/2 c water
3 clove garlic, crushed
1 star anise (available in oriental food section)
3 lb chicken parts
Cornstarch
Mandarin oranges

Combine first 8 ingredients in large pot. Bring to boil and add chicken. Simmer for 40 minutes until chicken is fully cooked. Remove chicken to serving platter. Remove and discard garlic and anise. Thicken shoyu brine with cornstarch mixed with water to desired thickness. Pour over chicken and garnish with mandarin oranges. Serve with rice.

Baked Ham with Guava Sherry Sauce

        1   Ham bone-in and scored (stud with cloves, optional)
        2   c 7-Up
        4   c guava nectar or juice
      1/2   c sweet sherry
        1   cinnamon stick
        3   whole cloves
      1/4   c guava jelly
        1   juice of lemon
        3   T cornstarch
        4   T water
            Salt and pepper to taste

Preheat oven to 375°.
Set studded ham in roasting pan and place in oven for about 10
minutes. Reduce temperature to 325°. Combine 7-Up with one cup guava
nectar. Baste the ham generously. Return ham to oven, basting every 15
minutes till mixture is used up. Continue baking until done using juices
in roasting pan for basting. Allow 10 minutes per pound.

Sauce:
Combine in saucepan the remaining guava juice, sherry, cinnamon
stick, cloves, guava jelly, lemon juice and the drippings from the ham.
Reduce till mixture is 3/4 of volume. Season and thicken with cornstarch and water. Strain and serve.

Barbecue Spareribs

        5   lbs spareribs
      2-3   pieces ginger
      3/4   c sugar
        1   c catsup
      3/4   c shoyu
      1/3   c oyster sauce
            Ajinomoto (optional)
            Sesame seeds

            continued...

Boil ribs and ginger in water for 1 hour and drain. Combine remaining ingredients except sesame seeds. Marinate ribs in sauce for 1 hour. Sprinkle with sesame seeds and broil or barbecue until done.

Serves 6-8

Beef Stroganoff

2	lbs sirloin, sliced 1/4" thick
1/2	c butter
2	c onion, coarsely chopped
2	cloves garlic, minced
1/2	lb mushrooms, sliced
2	T flour
	Salt and pepper
1 1/2	c bouillon or beef stock
1/4	c dry white wine
1	c sour cream
1	t Worcestershire sauce
	Handful of fresh parsley, chopped
1	lb dry fettuccine or 1 1/2 lbs fresh
2-3	T butter
	Fresh parsley, chopped

Brown strips of meat in butter. Remove from pan and keep warm. Add onion and garlic to pan and cook until tender. Add mushrooms and cook until tender. Stir flour into vegetables, season with salt and pepper to taste. Add bouillon and cook, stirring constantly, until thickened. Add white wine, sour cream, Worcestershire sauce and parsley. Mix in meat. Cook fettuccine in boiling, salted water 8-10 minutes for dry; 5-6 minutes for fresh. Drain and toss with butter. Serve meat on a bed of pasta. Sprinkle with parsley before serving.

Easy "Crock Pot" Pot Roast

- 5 lbs roast, cross rib, chuck or rump
- 2 cans cream of mushroom soup
- 1 can mushroom pieces
- 1/2 med onion, cut into 1" pieces
- 2-4 cloves garlic, sliced
- 1/2 c sour cream
  Salt & pepper

Place roast in crock pot or slow cooker. Add remaining ingredients and cover. Cook on low heat all day–about 8 hours. Delicious, tender, falls-off-the-fork roast!

Serve with mashed potatoes or egg noodles.

Mustard Crusted Leg of Lamb

- 1/2 c Dijon mustard
- 2 T shoyu
- 1 T brown sugar
- 2 cloves garlic, minced
- 1 t snipped fresh rosemary
- 1/4 t ground ginger
- 2 T olive oil
- 1 5-6 lb leg of lamb, bone in, skin removed

Place all ingredients except lamb in blender or food processor. Process to form thick paste. Spread mixture over lamb; cover and refrigerate 2 hours or overnight. Preheat oven to 350°. Place lamb on rack in shallow roasting pan. Insert meat thermometer into thickest portion of meat. Roast, uncovered, for 1 1/2 to 1 3/4 hours, or until thermometer registers 140° for medium rare. Cover and let stand 15 minutes before carving. (Temperature of meat will rise 5° during standing.)

Peachy Spareribs

5 lbs spareribs
1 c brown sugar
1 c catsup
4 T shoyu
4 t salt
4 t powdered ginger
4 sm jars of baby food peaches

Preheat oven to 400°. In a small saucepan, combine brown sugar, catsup, shoyu, salt, ginger and peaches. Cook over low heat until well blended and sugar is dissolved. Line 9"x13" pan with foil and put ribs in pan. Bake for 30 minutes. Drain drippings. Reduce oven to 325°. Pour sauce over ribs and bake approximately 1 hour or until meat is soft.

Popeye's Surprise

1 lb ground beef
2 10oz pkgs frozen chopped spinach
1 med onion, chopped
1 6oz can mushrooms
2 t garlic salt
1 t basil
1/4 c butter or margarine
1/4 c flour
1/2 t salt
2 c milk
2 c monterey jack cheese, grated

Preheat oven to 325°.
Brown beef and drain. Set aside in bowl. Cook spinach in the microwave for about 3 minutes; squeeze out excess moisture. In a saucepan, sauté onions until soft. Combine beef, spinach, onions, mushrooms, garlic salt and basil and place into casserole dish.
Melt butter or margarine in saucepan. Stir in flour and salt, mixing well. Slowly add milk and continue to stir until mixture is creamy. Pour over beef mixture. Top with cheese and bake uncovered for 30 minutes.

Serves 6-8

Quick Microwave Lasagna

1 box lasagna, cooked according to pkg directions, drained
32 oz jar spaghetti sauce
1 lb ground beef
3-4 Italian sausages, chopped
2 c ricotta cheese
1 egg, slightly beaten
2 T parsley, chopped
1/2 t pepper
8 slices mozzarella cheese
1/3 c parmesan cheese

Brown meats and drain. In a large saucepan, combine meats with spaghetti sauce. Simmer for 30 minutes. In a medium sized bowl, combine cheese, egg, parsley and pepper. Put 1/3 of the sauce on the bottom of a 9"x13" glass pan. Layer noodles on top, then 1/2 of ricotta mixture, then 1/2 of mozzarella cheese. Repeat sauce, noodles, ricotta and cheese. Add remaining sauce on top and sprinkle generously with parmesan cheese.

Cover pan with Saran wrap. Microwave 6 minutes on high, 20 minutes at 70% power. Let stand covered for 15 minutes to set.

Rafute (Shoyu Pork)

3-4 lbs pork shoulder
1 c pork stock or combination of pork and chicken stock
1 c bonito stock
1 c soy sauce
1 finger size chunk of ginger, sliced
1 c sugar
1 c awamori (Okinawan distilled rice spirit or sake)
1/2 c mirin

Place pork in a saucepan with water to cover. Bring to a boil and cook for 30 to 40 minutes. Remove pork from water, cool and slice into 1 1/2" squares.

Combine pork stock and bonito stock in saucepan. Add 1/2 c soy sauce and bring to a boil. Place pork and ginger slices in sauce and simmer, covered, for 1 1/2 hours over low heat. Add the remaining soy sauce, sugar and awamori. Continue to cook until pork becomes tender. As pork tenderizes, add mirin and cook for 1/2 hour, uncovered until pork is very tender.

Sausage Stuffed Meat Loaf with Gravy

      2 t unsalted butter
      1 lb ground beef
    1/2 lb ground pork
      1 c yellow onions, finely chopped
    1/2 c green bell peppers, finely chopped
      1 T garlic, minced
      2 lg eggs, slightly beaten
    1/2 c heavy cream
  1/2-1 c fine dried breadcrumbs (more for firmer meat loaf)
      1 t salt
    1/2 t freshly ground black pepper
      1 t Creole seasoning
    1/2 lb smoked chorizo sausage, chopped into 1/2" pieces
      1 c bottled chili sauce
      2 c veal stock or canned low-sodium beef broth
      2 T bleached all-purpose flour
         Mashed potatoes

Preheat oven to 350°. Grease a large roasting pan with butter. Combine beef, pork, onions, bell peppers, garlic, eggs, cream, breadcrumbs, salt, pepper, and Creole seasoning in a large mixing bowl and stir with a wooden spoon to mix. Pat half of the meat mixture into a rectangle about 9"x4" on the prepared pan. Layer the sausage on top of the loaf. Mold the remaining meat mixture around and over the sausage to cover it completely. Pour chili sauce on top. Bake, basting occasionally with the pan juices, for 1 1/2 hours. With a large spatula, carefully transfer the meat loaf to a serving platter.

Gravy:
Heat the roasting pan over high heat on the stovetop. Add veal stock, stir up the browned bits in the pan. Bring to a boil. Whisk flour and 2 tablespoons of water in a small bowl until smooth. Whisk flour mixture into the stock. Bring to a boil and cook, whisking often, until gravy thickens slightly, about 2 minutes. Season to taste. Serve meat loaf with hot mashed potatoes and gravy.

Simply Chili

1	lb lean ground meat
1	med onion, chopped
1	bell pepper, chopped
1	7oz Portuguese sausage, cut lengthwise and sliced
1	can kidney beans
2	cans whole tomatoes
2	cans tomato sauce
2	t salt
2	t pepper
2-3	T chili powder
2-10	shakes chili pepper flakes, to taste
2	bay leaves

In a large pot brown the ground meat. Drain and set aside. Heat oil and sauté onions and bell pepper. Add sausage and ground meat. Mix well. Stir in beans, tomatoes, tomato sauce and remaining ingredients. Adjust seasonings to taste. Simmer on low heat for 2-2 1/2 hours.

Spaghetti Carbonara

1/2 lb piece of pancetta (or bacon) cut into strips
4 cloves garlic, crushed
3 T extra virgin olive oil
1/4 c dry white wine
2 lg eggs
1/4 c romano, freshly grated
1/2 c parmigiano reggiano, freshly grated
   A liberal grinding of pepper
2 T parsley, chopped
1 lb cooked spaghetti, drained and hot

Put garlic in a small sauté pan with the olive oil and sauté until it turns deep gold. Remove the garlic from the pan and put in the strips of pancetta. Cook until edges become crisp. Add wine. Cook the wine down for 2 minutes. Remove from heat. Break the eggs into a serving bowl. Beat them lightly with a fork. Then add the cheeses, pepper and parsley. Mix thoroughly. Add drained, hot pasta to the bowl and toss rapidly to coat the strands well. Add the pancetta and wine mixture. Toss again and serve immediately.

Stuffed Cabbage

1 egg
1 t salt
   Dash pepper
1   t Worcestershire sauce
1/4 c onion, finely chopped
2/3 c milk
1 lb ground beef
1/2 lb ground pork
3/4 c rice, cooked
6 lg cabbage leaves
1 10 3/4oz can condensed tomato soup
1 T brown sugar
1 T lemon juice

continued...

Preheat oven to 350°. In a bowl combine egg, salt, pepper, Worcestershire sauce, onion, and milk; mix well. Add ground beef, ground pork and cooked rice; beat together with fork. Immerse cabbage leaves in boiling water for 3 minutes or just until limp; drain. Heavy center vein of leaf may be slit about 2 1/2 inches. Place 1/2 cup meat mixture on each leaf; fold in sides and roll ends over meat. Place rolls in 7 1/2"x12"x2" baking dish, flap side down. Blend together soup, brown sugar and lemon juice; pour over cabbage rolls. Bake for 1 1/4 hours. Baste once or twice with sauce.

Sweet and Sour Meatballs

  1 slice bread, torn into small pieces
  2 T milk
  1 lb lean ground beef
1/2 c green onion, chopped
  1 egg
  1 T shoyu
2/3 t salt
1/2 t dry mustard
  1 clove garlic, crushed
  2 T salad oil

Sauce: 1/2 c distilled white vinegar
        1/2 c sugar
          2 T cornstarch
          2 t shoyu

  1 8oz can pineapple chunks with juice

In a medium bowl, add bread pieces and milk. Toss. Stir in next 7 ingredients. Form into 1 1/2" balls. Brown in hot oil over medium-high heat, 5-7 minutes. Cover and cook on low heat about 3 minutes or until done. Drain and set aside. In large saucepan, combine vinegar, sugar, cornstarch and shoyu. Cook over medium heat until thick, stirring constantly. Stir in pineapple and add meatballs. Heat thoroughly. Serve over rice.

Veal Scallopini ala Marsala

2 lbs veal scallops
1/2 c flour
Salt and pepper
4 T butter
4 T oil
3 c mushrooms, sliced
Juice of 1 lemon
1/4 cup Marsala

Cover scallops with wax paper and pound with wooden mallet or cleaver until 1/8" thin.

Dredge meat in flour seasoned with salt and pepper. Combine butter and oil in skillet and brown veal on both sides. Add mushrooms and cook 10 minutes, stirring occasionally. Add lemon juice and Marsala and simmer 5 minutes more.

Aegean Shrimp Anita

1 onion, chopped
1/2 c olive oil
3/4 lb tomatoes, chopped
2 cloves garlic, crushed
1 sm bay leaf
1/2 t dried basil
1 t dried oregano
1/4 c fresh parsley, chopped
1/2 t hot sesame oil (do not omit)
Salt and freshly ground pepper to taste
3/4 -1 lb shrimp (raw, frozen or cooked)
1 small jar marinated artichoke hearts, drained
1/2 lb (8oz) feta cheese, crumbled
8 black olives, halved (preferably Greek olives)
1/2 lemon

In large skillet over medium-high heat, sauté onion in oil until soft. Add tomatoes, garlic, bay leaf, basil, oregano, parsley, hot sesame oil, salt and pepper. Cook 4 to 5 minutes. Remove vegetables from skillet with slotted spoon, leaving juices in skillet. Spread vegetables in bottom of an 8" square baking pan. Preheat oven to 475°. Bring pan juices to a boil; add shrimp and cook 2 minutes (don't overcook). Add shrimp mixture to baking pan. Add artichoke hearts and crumble feta over top. Arrange olives on top of feta and squeeze lemon over all. Bake 10 to 15 minutes. Serve over pasta.

Grilled Fresh Fish "Island Style"

1 c mayonnaise
2 T sesame oil
2 T green onion, chopped
1 lb white fish fillets
Salt and pepper
1/4 round onion, thinly sliced
4 lg mushrooms, sliced

Combine mayonnaise, oil and green onion; set aside. Slice fish fillets in half and grill quickly, searing both sides. Remove from grill and place on a large piece of aluminum foil. Season with salt and pepper. Lay onion and mushroom slices on each fillet and top with mayonnaise mixture. Close foil tightly and return to grill. (Foil packets may also be placed directly on coals, if desired.) Grill 15-30 minutes or until fish is flaky and opaque.

Hawaiian Halibut

2 cloves garlic, sliced
1/4 t ground white pepper
2 T sugar
1/3 c shoyu
6 T olive oil
3 green onions, chopped
1 T sesame seeds
6 halibut steaks, 1" thick

Combine all ingredients except halibut and stir well. Pour mixture over halibut and cover. Marinate in refrigerator overnight.
Grill approximately 7 minutes per side, until fish flakes easily.

Kamaaina Coconut Shrimp Curry

1 med onion, chopped
1/4 c butter or margarine
5 T flour
1 1/2 T curry powder
1 1/2 t brown sugar
2 cloves garlic, minced
1 small piece fresh ginger, minced
1 c chicken broth
2 c coconut milk
1 1/2 t salt
2 c cooked shrimp

Sauté onion in butter over medium heat. Stir in flour, curry powder, sugar, garlic and ginger. Cover and simmer for 1 hour on very low heat. Blend in broth and coconut milk, stirring until smooth. Cover and simmer for another hour. Caution! The sauce should not boil. Add salt and shrimp. Heat thoroughly and serve.

Orange Roughy Parmesan

2 lbs orange roughy fillets
   (any fresh, skinless white fish can be used)
2 T lemon juice
1/2 c parmesan cheese, grated
4 T butter, softened
3 T mayonnaise
3 T green onions, chopped
1/4 t salt
   Freshly ground pepper
   Dash Tabasco sauce

Preheat broiler. Place fillets in a buttered baking dish. Brush with lemon juice; let stand for 10 minutes. In a small bowl, combine cheese, butter, mayonnaise, green onions, salt, pepper and Tabasco sauce; set aside.

Broil fillets 3-4 minutes. Spread with cheese mixture and broil for an additional 2-3 minutes. Watch closely!

Salmon Baked in Puff Pastry with Truffles

Serves 6

1 lb puff pastry, defrosted
2 1/2 lb salmon fillets
2 T flat-leaf parsley, chopped
1 oz black truffles, sliced
3 hard boiled eggs, chopped
   Salt and pepper
1 egg, beaten (for egg wash)
2 bunches watercress, for garnish

Preheat oven to 375°. Cut pastry into 2 equal size pieces slightly larger than the salmon. Place 1 piece of pastry on oiled or parchment paper lined cookie sheet and set salmon on top of pastry sheet. Sprinkle with parsley. Lay truffles over salmon like scales trying to cover entire fish. Sprinkle eggs over truffles and season with salt and pepper. Place other piece of pastry on top. Seal edges and crimp with your fingers. Brush with egg wash and bake until pastry is golden brown, about 40 to 45 minutes. Let cool for 10 minutes. Slice into 6 equal size pieces, garnish platter or plate with watercress.

Seafood Pasta Casserole

1/2 lb shrimp, shelled and de-veined
1/2 lb scallops (halved if large)
1/4 c white wine
1 lb dry fettuccine or 1 1/2 lbs fresh

Béchamel Sauce:
1/2 c butter
1/2 c onion, chopped
1 clove garlic, crushed
1/2 c flour
2 t dry mustard
2 c milk
1 1/2 c light cream
1/2 t ground rosemary
1/4 t cayenne
1 t dried thyme
1 1/4 c swiss cheese, grated
1/4 c fresh parsley, chopped

Topping:
1/2 c pine nuts
1/4 c fresh parsley, chopped (for topping)

Preheat oven to 350°. Toss shrimp, scallops and white wine together and set aside. Cook fettuccine in salted boiling water (8-10 minutes for dry; 5-6 minutes for fresh). Drain and set aside. Sauté onion and garlic in butter until soft. Add flour and mustard and cook 1 minute, stirring constantly. Gradually add milk and light cream, stirring constantly until thickened. Add rosemary, cayenne and thyme to sauce and stir. Stir in cheese and parsley. Mix together pasta, seafood and sauce. Pour into large casserole. Sprinkle nuts and parsley over top. Bake for 30-35 minutes.

South Carolina Shrimp

      6 plum tomatoes
    1/4 c olive oil
     20 uncooked large shrimp, peeled and de-veined
      1 T shallot, minced
      1 T garlic, minced
    1/3 c dry white wine
    1/3 c fresh cilantro, chopped
      2 T fresh lemon juice
    1/2 c whipping cream
    3/4 stick of unsalted butter
         Salt and pepper
     12 oz fresh fettuccini, cooked

Peel, seed and chop tomatoes; set aside. Heat oil in large skillet and add shrimp. Sauté until pink. Transfer shrimp to a platter and set aside. Add shallot and garlic to skillet and sauté 1 minute. Add chopped tomatoes, wine, cilantro and lemon juice. Simmer until mixture is reduced by 1/2. Stir in cream and boil until mixture is again reduced by 1/2. Blend in butter and remove from heat; salt and pepper to taste. Place fettuccini on a serving plate. Lay shrimp on noodles and top with sauce.

West Coast Paella

1 1/2 lbs lg shrimp, uncooked
1/2 lb fresh scallops
2 dz clams
2 dz mussels
1 1/2 lbs chicken
1 t oregano
1 clove garlic, crushed
Salt and coarsely ground pepper, to taste
2 T olive oil
1 T wine vinegar
4 T oil
2 oz ham, sliced thin
2 oz hot sausage, preferably Spanish, sliced
1 lg onion, chopped
1 red bell pepper, chopped
1/2 t ground coriander
1/4 c tomato sauce
2 1/2 c long grain rice
4 c water
1 t saffron (threads only)
1 1/4 c fresh or frozen, thawed peas

Shell and de-vein shrimp and set aside. Wash mussels and clams well and set aside. Cut chicken into small serving pieces. Combine oregano, garlic, salt, pepper, olive oil, and vinegar and rub into chicken. In large, deep skillet, heat the 4 tablespoons of oil and brown chicken. Add ham, sausage, onion, bell pepper and coriander to chicken and cook 10 minutes. Stir in tomato sauce and rice and cook 4-5 minutes. In saucepan, bring water and saffron to a boil; then add, with shrimp, to chicken and cook covered until liquid is absorbed (about 20 minutes). Add peas and scallops and cook 5 minutes longer. Steam mussels and clams in a small amount of water just until the shells start to open. Add to paella mixture and serve hot.

Wine Poached Salmon with Pasta

- 3 T extra virgin olive oil
- 2 T butter or margarine
- 4 green onions; include 2 inches of the green tops minced
- 3 cloves garlic, minced
- 1/2 c dry white wine
- 3 T capers, rinsed
- 1 lb fresh salmon fillets, small bones picked out
- 3/4 lb farfalle pasta (small bow tie pasta)

Salt and fresh ground black pepper, to taste
Fresh parmesan cheese, grated

In a large sauté pan, sauté onions and garlic in the oil and butter just until they begin to color. Add wine and capers and bring to a simmer. Add the salmon fillets, cover and poach in the wine liquid, for about 5 minutes per half inch of thickness. When the salmon fillets are done, remove from heat, place the salmon and liquid (capers and all) in a large serving bowl and flake the salmon apart with two forks. In the meantime, cook the pasta in four quarts of boiling salted water until al dente. Drain pasta and add to salmon in the bowl. Toss well. Add salt and pepper. Serve on heated plates with sprinkle of fresh grated parmesan cheese.

Antipasto Lasagna

1   27 1/2oz jar fat-free mushroom and
        roasted garlic tomato pasta sauce
1   box lasagna
1   14oz can artichoke hearts, not marinated
1   12oz bottle roasted bell peppers
1   c tofu, cubed
1/2 c kalamata olives, pitted and sliced
        Shredded mozzarella
        (as much or as little as you want, but at least 1 cup)

Preheat oven to 450°. Cook pasta according to package directions. Prepare 9"x13" baking dish with cooking spray. Spread 1/2 cup of pasta sauce onto bottom of pan. Arrange a layer of pasta over sauce; top with half of the artichokes, tofu and olives. Sprinkle with cheese and top with 3/4 cup sauce. Repeat layers, ending with remainder of sauce. Cover and bake for 30 minutes. Let stand for 5 minutes before serving.

Chili Relleno Casserole

1   8oz can Ortega green chilies
1/2 lb monterey jack cheese
2   eggs
2   T flour
1   15oz can evaporated milk
1/2 lb cheddar cheese, shredded
1   c red salsa

Preheat oven to 350°. Split chilies length-wise and discard seeds and veins. Rinse in cold water. Line bottom of a 9" square casserole with opened chilies. Sprinkle monterey jack cheese on chilies. Place another layer of chilies on top of cheese.

Blend eggs, flour and milk together. Pour over chilies. Sprinkle cheddar cheese on top. Bake for 30 minutes and top with salsa.

Linguine with Brie and Tomatoes

    4   ripe lg tomatoes, cut into 1/2 inch cubes
    1   lb brie cheese, rind removed and torn into irregular pieces
    1   c fresh basil leaves, cleaned and cut into strips
    3   cloves garlic, peeled and finely minced
    1   c plus 1 T best quality olive oil
2 1/2   t salt
  1/2   t freshly ground black pepper
1 1/2   lbs linguine
        Freshly grated imported parmesan cheese (optional)

Combine tomatoes, brie, basil, garlic, 1 cup olive oil, 1/2 teaspoon each salt and pepper in a large serving bowl. Prepare at least 2 hours before serving and set aside, covered, at room temperature.

Bring 6 quarts water to a boil in a large pot. Add 1 tablespoon olive oil and remaining salt. Add linguine and boil until tender but still firm, 8-10 minutes.

Drain pasta and immediately toss with the tomato mixture. Serve at once. Garnish with parmesan cheese if desired.

Tofu Steak with Three Colored Bell Peppers

- 1 block firm tofu sliced in thirds
   Flour for dusting
   Vegetable oil for frying
   Unsalted butter for sautéing
- 1/2 c soy sauce
- 1/2 c mirin (sweet sake)
- 1 med size onion, peeled and cut
- 1/2 oz ginger, peeled and sliced
- 1 each, bell peppers (red, yellow and orange), julienne
- 1 pack enoki mushroom cleaned
- 1 scallion, finely chopped

In an electric blender combine soy sauce, mirin, onion and ginger. Blend for 30 seconds, until smooth, and set aside. Dust tofu with flour. In a large frying pan heat vegetable oil and fry tofu until light brown on both sides. Remove from heat. In frying pan melt butter, add mushrooms and bell peppers and sauté until mushrooms wilt, set aside and keep warm. Place tofu slices on medium serving plate. Pour sauce over tofu and top with bell pepper mixture. Sprinkle with scallions. Serve immediately.

Triple Cheese Manicotti

8 lg manicotti shells
1 t vegetable oil or olive oil
1/2 onion, chopped
2 cloves garlic, crushed
1/2 c bell pepper, chopped
2 c tomato sauce
1/2 t basil
1/2 t oregano
1/2 t thyme
1/4 t fresh ground black pepper
1 1/2 c mozzarella, shredded
1 c low fat cottage cheese or ricotta cheese
1/3 c parmesan cheese, grated
2 eggs, beaten

Cook manicotti shells according the package directions. Drain. Heat oil in large saucepan and sauté onion, garlic and bell pepper until onions are translucent. Stir in tomato sauce, basil, oregano, thyme and pepper. Cover and let simmer 20 minutes. Remove from heat. Combine one cup mozzarella with cottage cheese, parmesan cheese and beaten eggs and stir well.

Preheat oven to 350°.

Stuff cheese mix into cooked shells, using 1/4 cup per shell (approx.). Pour 1/2 of tomato sauce mix into shallow 2-quart casserole. Arrange stuffed shells on top and pour remaining sauce over. Sprinkle with remaining mozzarella. Bake uncovered for 1/2 hour or until bubbly.

Vegetarian Chili

1	c lentils
1	c kidney beans (or 15 oz can)
1	c garbanzo beans (or 15 oz can)
1	onion, chopped
2	cloves garlic, minced
3	T olive oil
5-6	c water
2	carrots, chopped
2	celery stalks, chopped
2	8oz cans tomato sauce
1	can stewed tomatoes
1	bay leaf
1	T chili powder
2	T flour
	Salt and pepper to taste

Soak lentils according to package directions. Soak kidney and garbanzo beans separately. (If using canned beans, drain and set aside). In a large pot sauté onion and garlic in olive oil until transparent. Add water, carrots, celery, tomato sauce, stewed tomatoes, bay leaf and drained beans. Mix chili powder and flour together then add to above. Season with salt and pepper. Simmer for 1 hour.

Desserts

Desserts

Baked Apple Pudding

2   c sugar
1/2 c butter or margarine, softened
2   eggs, beaten
6   apples (peeled and chopped)
2   c flour
2   t baking soda
1   t nutmeg
1   t cinnamon
    Pinch salt
1   c chopped nuts (if desired)

Preheat oven to 325°. Cream together sugar and butter until creamy. Add remaining ingredients and blend well. Pour into a greased casserole dish and bake for 45 minutes.

Sauce: 1   c butter
         1   c brown sugar
         1   c cream
         2   heaping T flour
         1   t vanilla

Combine sauce ingredients in saucepan. Stir over low heat until smooth. Serve warm over Baked Apple Pudding.

Banana Cream Squares

Crust: 1 1/2 c butter
    1 1/2 c flour
      3 T powdered sugar, sifted
     3/4 c chopped nuts (optional)

Preheat oven to 350°. In a 9"x13" baking pan, melt butter. Combine remaining ingredients. Spread and press evenly into pan. Bake for 15 minutes. Cool when done.

Filling: 1 8oz cream cheese
          3 c milk
          2 pkg instant vanilla pudding
          6 lg bananas
          2 c Cool Whip

Beat cream cheese, milk and pudding for 3 minutes. Slice banana into 1/2" pieces. Spread bananas evenly on crust. Spread mixture over bananas. Refrigerate for at least one hour. Top with Cool Whip. Garnish with extra chopped nuts and banana slices, if desired.

Best Cookie Recipe

  1   stick unsalted butter, softened
  1   stick margarine, softened
  1   c sugar
  1   c light brown sugar, firmly packed
  2   t vanilla
  3/4 c vegetable oil
  1   egg
3 1/2 c all purpose flour
  1   t salt
  1   t baking soda
  1   t cream of tartar
  1   c finely chopped nuts
  1   c old-fashioned quaker oats (not quick cooking)
  1   c shredded coconut (can be toasted if you wish)
  1   c Rice Krispies

Preheat oven to 325°. In mixing bowl, cream butter and margarine. Add sugars, vanilla, and oil. Beat until smooth. Add egg and beat again until smooth. Add flour, salt, baking soda, and cream of tartar. Add nuts, oats, coconut and rice krispies. Fold in until well blended. Cover bowl with saran wrap and refrigerate for 1 hour or more. Dough will be stiff enough to handle. Spray cookie sheets lightly. Pinch off teaspoon-size pieces and flatten with fingers. Place on cookie sheet. Bake for 10 minutes. After removing from oven, leave cookies on the cookie sheets for a few minutes. Cool on racks.

Bittersweet Chocolate Dessert Sauce

1/3 c sugar
1/3 c water
2 sq unsweetened chocolate
2 sq semi-sweet chocolate
2 T butter
1/8 t salt
3/4 t vanilla

In a heavy 1 qt saucepan, heat all ingredients except vanilla to boiling, stirring frequently (mixture will look separated). Reduce heat to medium-low, simmer uncovered until smooth and thickened, about 3 minutes, stirring constantly. Remove from heat and stir in vanilla. Serve as topping for ice cream, cake or fruit.

Bread Pudding

1 lb loaf sweet bread, torn into pieces
1/2 c raisins, split into 1/4 c
1/2 c shredded coconut, split into 1/4 c
4 t cinnamon, split into 2 t
3 c milk
1 c sugar
4 eggs
2 t vanilla
2 sticks butter

Preheat oven to 350°. Place 1/2 of sweet bread pieces in a 9"x13" roasting pan. Sprinkle 1/4 c raisins, 1/4 c coconut and 2 t cinnamon onto bread pieces. Continue layering with the remaining sweetbread, raisins, cinnamon, and coconut. In a large mixing bowl, combine the milk, sugar, eggs and vanilla. Mix well. Pour evenly over the sweetbread. Dot with butter. Place in oven for 1 hour exactly–less will result in "wet" bread pudding, more will result in "dry" bread pudding.

Serves 6

Burnt Cream

2 c whipping cream
4 egg yolks
1/2 c sugar
1 T vanilla
Sugar for topping

Preheat oven to 350°. Heat cream over low heat until bubbles form around edges of saucepan. In separate bowl beat egg yolks and sugar together until thick, about 3 minutes. Gradually beat cream into egg yolk. Stir in vanilla and pour into 6 6oz custard cups. Place custard cups in baking pan that has about 1/2 inch water on the bottom. Bake until set, about 45 minutes. Remove custard cups from water and refrigerate until chilled. Sprinkle each custard with about 2 t sugar. Place on top rack under broiler and cook until topping is medium brown. Chill before serving.

Serves 6-8

Buttermilk Pound Cake

1 c butter (or Crisco)
3 c sugar
5 eggs
2 t vanilla
1/2 t baking soda
1 c buttermilk
3 c flour

Preheat oven to 325°. Grease a bundt pan. Cream butter with sugar gradually. Add eggs, one at a time, beating each time; add vanilla. Combine baking soda with the buttermilk; set aside.

Combine flour and buttermilk mixture, add to butter cream slowly. Pour into bundt pan and bake 1-1 1/2 hours.

Chocolate Pecan Pie

Crust: 1 T softened butter
         3/4 c pecans, finely chopped

Filling: 1/2 c dark corn syrup
          2 eggs, slightly beaten
         1/4 t salt
          1 t vanilla
          1 c semi-sweet chocolate bits

Garnish:
         1/2 c pecans, coarsely broken

Preheat oven to 350°. Butter an 8" pie pan with softened butter and press in the chopped nuts. Combine syrup, eggs, salt and vanilla and beat well. Melt chocolate bits over hot water and add them slowly to the syrup mixture, stirring constantly. Pour into pie shell and garnish with pecans. Bake for 25-30 minutes. Serve with vanilla-flavored whipped cream.

Chocolate Walnut Crumb Bars

        1   c (2 sticks) butter, softened
        2   c flour
      1/2   c sugar
      1/4   t salt
        2   c (12oz pkg) chocolate chips, divided
   1 1/4   c (14oz can) sweetened condensed milk
        1   t vanilla
        1   c walnuts, chopped

Preheat oven to 350°. Beat butter in large mixing bowl until creamy. Add flour, sugar and salt and mix until crumbly. With floured fingers, press 2 cups crumb mixture onto bottom of greased 9"x13" baking pan; reserve remaining mixture. Bake for 10 to 12 minutes until edges are golden brown. Warm 1 1/2 cups chocolate chips and sweetened condensed milk in small, heavy saucepan over low heat, stirring until smooth. Stir in vanilla. Spread chocolate mixture over hot crust. Stir walnuts and remaining chocolate chips into reserved crumb mixture; sprinkle over chocolate filling. Bake for 25 to 30 minutes until center is set. Cool in pan on wire rack. Cut with sharp knife into bars.

Coconut Mochi

        1   box mochiko
   2 1/2   c sugar
        2   c water
        1   can frozen coconut milk, thawed
        1   t baking powder
        1   t vanilla
            Few drops of red food coloring
            Potato starch (katakuriko), for dusting

Preheat oven to 350°. In a large mixing bowl, blend together mochiko, sugar and water. Add rest of ingredients except potato starch. Pour into greased 9"x13" pan. Cover with foil and bake for 1 hour. Cool for 30 minutes. Cut into desired pieces and dust with potato starch.

Decadent Chocolate Cake

1 box Duncan Hines devil's food chocolate cake mix
1 box instant chocolate pudding
2 c sour cream
6 T kahlua
1 t vanilla
4 eggs
1/2 c oil
1 c chocolate chips

Preheat oven to 300°. Mix together all above ingredients adding eggs one at a time. Pour into greased and floured bundt pan. Bake for 1 hour. Cool cake in pan for 20 minutes before removing from pan. Before serving dust powdered sugar on top of cake.

Double Fudge Chocolate Cake

2 eggs
1 c sugar
2 T butter, softened
1 c light oil
1/2 c cocoa, packed
1/2 c buttermilk
1 t vanilla

Preheat oven to 350°. In large bowl, add above ingredients one at a time in order, beating after each addition. Set aside.

2 1/4 c flour
1 1/2 t baking soda
1 1/2 t baking powder
1 c boiling water
1/2 c chocolate chips

In separate bowl, sift together dry ingredients. Add dry ingredients to eggs and sugar mixture. Fold in the boiling water, and add chocolate chips. Place mixture in greased and floured 9"x13" cake pan (or 2 - 8" round cake pans). Bake for 30-35 minutes. Test for doneness with a toothpick. Cool completely. Ice with Incredible Chocolate Icing.

Incredible Chocolate Icing:
1 c butter, softened
2 c powdered sugar
1 1/3 c cocoa
2 t vanilla
1/4 c milk
1/4 c hot coffee

Place butter, sugar and cocoa in blender or food processor and blend for a few seconds. Add liquids and blend until smooth. For thinner icing, use additional milk.

Frango Mint Brownies

1 2oz bar baking chocolate
1/2 c butter
2 eggs
1 c sugar
1 t vanilla
1/2 c flour
   Pinch salt
1/2 c pecans, chopped
1/2 c Frango mints, chopped

Preheat oven to 350°. Grease an 8" square pan. Melt chocolate and butter in double boiler or microwave. Beat eggs until lemon colored in large bowl. Add sugar gradually to eggs and beat until smooth and light. Stir in melted chocolate mixture and vanilla. Sift flour and salt in separate bowl and add to batter. Fold in pecans and Frango mints. Pour into prepared pan and bake 20-25 minutes–avoid overbaking. Cool and cut into 2" squares.

Frosted Butterscotch Cookies

     1 1/2 c brown sugar, firmly packed
       1/2 c shortening
         2 eggs, slightly beaten
         1 t vanilla
         1 c sour cream
     2 1/2 c flour
         1 t baking soda
       1/2 t baking powder
       1/2 t salt
       2/3 c walnuts, chopped

Preheat oven to 375°. In large mixing bowl, cream together sugar, shortening, eggs, vanilla and sour cream. Add dry ingredients and walnuts, mixing well. Drop batter on ungreased cookie sheet by teaspoon. Bake for 10 to 12 minutes. Cool on rack.

Frosting:
       1/2 c butter
     3 1/2 c powdered sugar
     1 1/2 t vanilla
       5-6 t hot water

Melt butter slowly in sauce pan. Add sugar, vanilla and water. Beat until easy to spread. Frost cooled cookies immediately.

Frozen Lime Pie

Crust: 1 1/2 c graham cracker crumbs
       1/3 c powdered sugar
       1/4 c butter, softened

Filling: 2 eggs
       1/2 c sugar
            Green food coloring
         1 c light cream
       1/3 c lime juice
         1 T grated lime peel
         1 pint vanilla ice cream

Combine graham cracker crumbs, powdered sugar and butter. Mix until moist and blended. Press cracker crumbs into lightly greased 9" pie pan (reserve 1/4 cup mixture for top of pie). Chill pie crust. Beat eggs until thick and lemon colored. Gradually add sugar and continue beating until light and fluffy. Add a few drops of green food coloring, cream, lime juice and peel. Mix well. Pour into freezing tray and freeze until firm. Break into chunks. Turn into chilled bowl, beat smooth. Return to cold tray and partially freeze. Whip ice cream until smooth. Spread into pie crust. Top with partly frozen lime mixture. Sprinkle with extra crumbs and freeze until firm.

Gingersnap Cookies

      1/2 c sugar
      1/2 c dark brown sugar, firmly packed
        1 c sweet butter, softened
        1 egg
      1/3 c dark molasses
        2 t ground ginger
      1/2 t allspice
        1 t cinnamon
        2 t baking soda
      1/2 t salt
      1/4 t ground white pepper
    2 1/4 c flour
           Brown crystallized sugar (for topping)

   Preheat oven to 325°. Cream the sugars and butter in bowl with
mixer until light and fluffy. Beat in egg and molasses. Add dry ingredients and blend well. Chill dough for 1 hour. Roll into balls and roll in
crystallized sugar. Place on cookie sheet 2-3 inches apart. Flatten
slightly with fingers. Bake 12 minutes.

Haupia Squares

Crust: 3/4 c butter or margarine, softened
            4 T sugar
      1 1/2 c flour
        1/2 c nuts, chopped
               Pinch of salt

Haupia Layer:
        7 T cornstarch
      1/2 c water
        2 cans frozen coconut milk, thawed
      3/4 c sugar
        1 c water
        1 8oz carton Cool Whip

      continued...

Grated coconut
Chopped nuts

Preheat oven to 350°. Combine crust ingredients and press into a 9"x13" baking pan. Bake for 20 minutes and cool. Dissolve cornstarch in 1/2 c of water. Pour into saucepan and add coconut milk, sugar and 1 c of water. Cook until thickened. (Use a wooden spoon for stirring as metal spoons discolor the coconut) Cool. Pour into crust and chill until firm. Spread with Cool Whip and sprinkle coconut and nuts on top.

Serves 15-20

Hawaiian Pineapple Cake

Cake:
2 c sugar
2 c flour
2 t baking soda
2 eggs
1 20oz can crushed pineapple, undrained
1 c walnuts, chopped

Icing:
8 oz cream cheese, softened
1/4 c butter or margarine, softened
1 t vanilla
1 3/4 c powdered sugar

Preheat oven to 350°. Combine all cake ingredients in large bowl. Pour into greased 9"x13" baking pan. Bake 40-45 minutes and cool completely.
Cream icing ingredients together. Spread onto cooled cake.

Hawaiian Shortbread

1 lb butter, softened
1 c sugar
4 c flour
2 t vanilla
1 c unsweetened coconut (finely grated or shredded)

In large mixing bowl cream together the butter and sugar. Add flour, vanilla and coconut. Mix well and chill overnight. Preheat oven to 325°. Spread into 9"x13" baking pan and bake for 15 minutes. Cool and cut into squares.

Kahlua Toffee Trifle

1 9"x13" dark chocolate sheet cake, prepared
4 c chocolate pudding, prepared
1 12oz Cool Whip, thawed
6 1.4oz English toffee candy bars
1/2 c Kahlua liqueur

Cut 1/2 the cake in large pieces and place in bottom of large salad bowl or punchbowl. Pour 1/4 c Kahlua over cake and pat down. Layer pudding over cake. Layer 1/2 whipped topping over pudding. Crush 3 toffee bars and sprinkle over whipped topping. Repeat layers. Chill and serve.

Serves 10-12

Lemon Bundt Cake

1 pkg yellow cake mix
4 eggs
3/4 c oil
3/4 c water
1/4 t butter flavoring
    Few drops of yellow coloring
1 pkg lemon jello

Preheat oven to 350°. Mix all above ingredients. Beat for 1 minute. Pour into greased and floured bundt pan. Bake for 50-60 minutes. Test for doneness with a toothpick.

Lemon Glaze:
    Juice of 1 lemon
    Grated rind of 1 lemon
6 T butter
6 T sugar

In a small saucepan combine all glaze ingredients and bring to a boil. Pour over cake immediately after removing it from the oven. Let cake cool for 20 minutes before removing from pan.

Lilikoi Meringue Pie

   1 c sugar
1/4 c cornstarch
1/2 c water
   2 egg yolks, slightly beaten
   2 T butter or margarine
   1 12oz can passion fruit juice
   2 drops yellow food coloring, if desired
   1 9" pie shell, baked

Meringue:
   3 egg whites
1/4 t cream of tartar
   6 T sugar
1/2 t vanilla

Preheat oven to 400°. Mix sugar and cornstarch in medium saucepan. Gradually stir in water. Cook over medium heat, stirring constantly, until mixture thickens and boils. Boil and stir 1 minute. Gradually stir in half the hot mixture into beaten egg yolks. Blend into hot mixture in pan, boil and stir 1 minute. Remove from heat, stir in butter, juice and food coloring. Pour into baked pie shell. In a medium mixing bowl, beat egg whites and cream of tartar until foamy. Beat in sugar, 1 tablespoon at a time. Continue beating until stiff and glossy. Do not underbeat. Add vanilla. Heap onto hot pie filling; spread carefully sealing to edge of crust. Bake 10 minutes until golden brown. Cool away from draft.

Lovely Meringues

        3 egg whites
           Pinch of salt
        1 c sugar
      3/4 c semi-sweet chocolate chips
        2 T unsweetened cocoa
      1/2 t vanilla

   Preheat oven to 375°. Line cookie sheets with parchment paper or foil. In medium sized mixing bowl, beat egg whites and salt until peaks start to form. Gradually beat in sugar until egg whites are stiff enough to hold their shape. Stir in chips, cocoa powder and vanilla. Drop batter by tablespoon onto cookie sheets. Bake 35 minutes. Transfer foil sheet to rack and cool. Remove carefully from foil. Store in an airtight container.

Malasadas

        1 pkg dry yeast
        1 t sugar
      1/4 c warm water
        6 eggs
        6 c flour
      1/4 t lemon extract
      1/2 c sugar
      1/4 c butter, melted
        1 c evaporated milk
        1 c water
        1 t salt
           Sugar for coating

   Dissolve yeast and sugar in warm water. Set aside. In a small bowl beat eggs until thick. Put flour in large bowl, make well in center. Add yeast mixture into eggs and add lemon extract, sugar, butter, milk, water and salt. Add to flour in large bowl. Mix thoroughly to form a soft dough. Cover and let rise until double. In deep fat, drop dough by spoonfuls, fry until brown. Drain and roll in sugar.

Mango Bars

Crust: 2 c flour
          1/2 c sugar
          1 c butter, softened

Filling: 4 c mangoes, chopped
          3/4 c sugar
          1/3 c water
          1 t lemon juice
          1 t vanilla
          1 t cinnamon
          3 T cornstarch
          3 T water

Topping: 2 c quick oats
          1/4 c flour
          1/2 c sugar
          2/3 c butter, softened

Preheat oven to 350°. Grease 9"x13" baking pan. Combine flour with sugar. Add butter and press into prepared baking pan; bake 7 minutes. Combine mangoes, sugar, water, lemon juice, vanilla and cinnamon in a saucepan. Simmer until the mangoes are tender, about 10 minutes. Combine cornstarch and water; stir into the mango mixture and cook until thickened. Remove from heat and cool slightly. Pour over prepared crust. Combine oats, flour and sugar. Blend in butter and sprinkle over mango mixture. Bake for 50 minutes, cool and cut into bars. Store in refrigerator.

Neiman Marcus Brownies

    1 box yellow cake mix
  1/2 c butter, melted
    3 eggs
    1 c semi-sweet chocolate chips
    1 c pecans, chopped
  1/2 c coconut, shredded (optional)
    1 8oz pkg cream cheese, softened
    1 lb box powdered sugar

Preheat oven to 325°. Grease a glass 9"x13" baking pan.

In a large bowl combine cake mix, butter and one of the eggs. Press into prepared pan. Sprinkle chocolate chips, pecans and coconut over cake mixture; set aside.

In a medium bowl, combine cream cheese, powdered sugar and remaining 2 eggs; mix well. Pour this mixture over the cake and chips. Bake for 40-50 minutes. Do not overbake; cool and slice.

Oatmeal Cake

- 1/4 c butter, softened
- 1 c brown sugar, firmly packed
- 1 c granulated sugar
- 1 c oatmeal cereal, prepared
- 2 eggs
- 1 t vanilla
- 1 t cinnamon
- 1 t soda
- 1/2 t salt
- 1 1/3 c flour

Preheat oven to 350°. In a large mixing bowl cream butter and sugars together. Add in remaining ingredients and mix well. Pour into 9"x13" greased baking pan. Bake for 30-35 minutes.

Topping:
- 1 T butter
- 1 c brown sugar, firmly packed
- 1 can evaporated milk
- 1 c coconut, shredded

In saucepan, melt butter, stir in brown sugar and milk. When blended, remove from heat, add coconut and mix well. Pour over cake, as soon as cake is removed from oven. Broil until mixture is bubbly and lightly toasted. Cool and eat!

Oreo Smash Hit

- 1/2 gallon vanilla ice cream, softened

Crust:
- 1 lg pkg oreo cookies, crushed
- 1/2 c (1 stick) butter or margarine, melted

Press crushed cookies into a 9"x13" baking pan. Drizzle butter evenly over crumbled cookies. Freeze for 1 hour.
Spread softened ice cream over frozen crust and return to freezer.

continued...

Sauce:
- 1 c sugar
- 2 sq unsweetened chocolate
- 1/2 c (1 stick) butter or margarine
- 1 c evaporated milk

Bring sauce ingredients to a boil for 10 minutes in a saucepan, stirring often. Remove from heat. When cooled completely, pour sauce evenly over firm ice cream. Cover and return to freezer for at least 2 hours before serving.

Pineapple Upside Down Cake

- 1 pkg yellow cake mix
- 1 pkg instant vanilla pudding
- 4 eggs
- 1 c water
- 1/2 c oil

Topping:
- 1/2 c (1 stick) butter, melted
- 1/2 c brown sugar
- 1 15oz can pineapple, crushed or sliced, drained

Preheat oven to 350°. Put all cake ingredients in large bowl—beat until well blended. In separate bowl, mix butter and sugar well. Pour into 9"x13" pan and spread evenly. Arrange pineapple on top of butter mixture. Pour cake mixture over pineapple. Bake 35-40 minutes. When cake is done, cool for 10-15 minutes. Turn cake over onto cookie sheet or large platter.

Praline Cheesecake

Crust: 1 1/2 c graham crackers crumbs
3 T sugar
3 T butter, melted

Filling: 3 8oz pkgs cream cheese
3/4 c brown sugar
2 T flour
3 eggs
2 T vanilla
1/2 c pecans, chopped
1/2 c whipping cream, whipped
Maple syrup
12–14 whole pecans

In a medium bowl, combine crust ingredients with a fork until crumbly. Press mixture into the bottom of a 9" spring-form pan. Chill.
Preheat oven to 450°. In a large bowl, combine cream cheese, sugar, flour, eggs, vanilla and chopped pecans; mix until smooth. Fold in whipped cream and pour mixture over crust. Bake for 10 minutes. Reduce heat to 250° and bake 30-40 minutes longer. Chill overnight. Remove cheesecake from pan. Brush top with maple syrup and garnish with a pecan on each slice.

Seven Layer Cookies

1/2 c butter, melted
1 c graham cracker crumbs
1 c shredded coconut
1 c chocolate chips
1 c butterscotch chips
1 c walnuts or pecans, finely chopped
1 14oz can sweetened condensed milk

continued...

Preheat oven to 325°. Spray 9"x13" pan with cooking spray. Layer ingredients in order listed above ending with condensed milk drizzled over all. Bake for 30 minutes. Cut while still warm. Chill well before removing from pan.

White Chocolate Mousse

       12 oz white chocolate
        3 c heavy cream
        2 egg yolks
        2 whole eggs
      3/4 c sugar
    1 1/2 T unflavored gelatin

Chop white chocolate into small pieces and melt in double boiler over hot water. Cool. Whip heavy cream until stiff, then refrigerate. Beat egg yolks and whole eggs together. Add sugar and beat until a light lemon color. Stir a little of egg mixture into gelatin then add back to remaining eggs and mix thoroughly. Beat melted white chocolate slowly into egg and gelatin mixture. Fold in whipped cream. Place in 8-cup mold and chill for 2 hours.

Dark chocolate layer:
       24 oz semi-sweet chocolate
    1 1/2 c heavy cream
        5 T sugar
        3 T butter
        2 T Grand Marnier

Chop semi-sweet chocolate into small bits. In saucepan combine heavy cream, sugar and butter. Bring to a boil. Remove from heat. Add chocolate and mix until blended. Cool at room temperature for 2 hours. Add Grand Marnier. Pour over top of white chocolate mold. Refrigerate 4 hours. Dip mold in warm water. Turn onto serving dish.

World's Best Peanut Butter Cookies

1 c margarine or butter
1 c peanut butter
1 c sugar
1 c brown sugar, firmly packed
2 eggs
2 c flour
1 t baking soda
1 6oz pkg semi-sweet chocolate pieces
1/2 c roasted peanuts, chopped

Preheat oven to 350°. Cream margarine and peanut butter. Gradually add sugar until blended. Add eggs, one at a time while beating until smooth. Set aside. In separate bowl, sift flour and baking soda. Gradually add dry ingredients to creamed mixture. Stir in chocolate and peanuts. Drop by teaspoonful onto greased baking sheets and flatten slightly using the back of spoon. Bake for 15-20 minutes.

Yummy Cheese Pie

12 oz cream cheese
2 eggs
1/2 c sugar
1 t vanilla
1 #2 can crushed pineapple (or pie topping of preference)
1 graham cracker crust pie shell

Preheat oven to 350°. Beat all together except pineapple (topping) and pour into graham cracker crust. Bake for 20 minutes; cool. Add pineapple (topping) and chill.

Zesty Lemon Squares

Crust:
- 2 c flour
- 1/2 c powdered sugar
- 1 c butter

Preheat oven to 350°. Mix above ingredients in food processor. Pack mixture in bottom and sides of 9"x13" ungreased pan. Bake for 15 minutes until edges are golden brown.

Filling:
- 4 eggs
- 2 c sugar
- 2 t powdered sugar
- 1/3 c lemon juice
- Rind of lemon, grated
- 1/4 c flour
- 1/2 t baking powder
- Pinch salt

Beat eggs, sugar, powdered sugar, lemon juice and lemon rind. Set aside. Sift together flour, baking powder and salt. Combine with lemon mixture. Pour filling mixture over crust and bake 25-30 minutes. Let stand and cool for 2 hours before cutting into squares. Sprinkle with powdered sugar.

Marinades
&
Sauces

Marinades & Sauces

Basil and Parsley Sauce (for fish)

1/2 c white wine
1/4 c lemon juice
  1 c heavy cream
1/4 c fresh parsley, chopped
1/4 c fresh basil, finely chopped
  1 T capers
     Salt and pepper to taste

Combine wine and lemon juice in medium saucepan and cook on medium heat for 2-3 minutes. Add cream and cook until liquid is reduced by half (3/4 cup). Add parsley, basil, capers, salt and pepper to taste and whisk until well blended. Remove from heat.
Enough sauce to pour over 2 lbs of any fish fillets.

Creole Sauce

1/4 c onion, finely chopped
  3 T green pepper, finely chopped
  1 T butter
  1 8oz can tomato sauce
  1 3oz can chopped mushrooms, drained
1/4 c water
     Dash of pepper
     Dash of garlic salt

Cook onion and green pepper in butter until tender. Add remaining ingredients. Cover and simmer 15 minutes. Serve with fish.

Dad's Secret Steak Marinade

Makes 1½ cups

1/4 c vegetable oil
2 T shoyu
2 T Mirin wine
1 T steak sauce
2 T oyster sauce
3/4 c brown sugar
2 T Hawaiian salt

Place first 5 ingredients in a baking pan and mix thoroughly. Rub sauce onto steak on both sides and ends.

Rub brown sugar over the steaks and sprinkle with salt. Marinate for 1 hour.

Easy BBQ Sauce

Makes 4 cups

2 c catsup
2 c water
1 onion, finely chopped
3 T prepared mustard
1 t chili powder (more to taste)
6 T brown sugar

Combine all ingredients and simmer over medium heat until blended well. Use on your favorite barbecued meat or to zest up meat loaf.

Hawaiian Mango Chutney

- 1 qt cider vinegar
- 7 c sugar
- 1 c raisins
- 1 c dried currants
- 1 c ginger, chopped
- 2-4 Hawaiian chili peppers, chopped and seeded
- 5 cloves garlic, whole
- 3 T salt
- 4 cloves
- 1/2 t allspice
- Juice of 1 lemon
- 10 c ripe mango, sliced

Combine all ingredients, except mango, in a large heavy saucepan; mix well. Bring to a boil, and continue to boil gently for about 45 minutes. Stir frequently. Add mango and simmer until glazed; approximately 10 minutes. Cool, store in jars and refrigerate. Keeps for many months.

Honey Garlic Sauce (for ribs)

- 1 1/2 c honey
- 1 c water
- 1 t garlic, crushed
- 1 T Worcestershire sauce
- 1 T tomato paste
- 2 drops Tabasco sauce
- 1/2 T powdered ginger
- 2 T cornstarch
- 1/4 c cold water

Combine all ingredients except cornstarch and 1/4 cup cold water in saucepan. Heat to boiling. In small bowl, dissolve cornstarch in the cold water; add to sauce, mixing well. Cook on medium heat, stirring constantly until smooth and thickened. Pour over ribs before broiling or roasting.

Li Hing Mui Pickled Mango

        6   qts mango slices

Marinade:
        2   c cider vinegar
        5   c brown sugar
    1/2   c Hawaiian salt
        6   c water
    1/2   t Chinese five spice
        1   lg pkg seedless li hing mui

Place mango slices in jars. Boil marinade ingredients except li hing mui. Cool, then add li hing mui. Pour over mango slices. Store in refrigerator. Ready to eat in 3 days.
Note: Any kind of mango can be used.

Makes 2 cups

Mango Salsa

        1   lg mango, peeled, pitted and diced
        3   T onion, chopped
        3   T green bell pepper, chopped
        3   T red bell pepper, chopped
        1   t fresh chives, minced
    1 1/2   T white wine vinegar
        1   T fresh cilantro, chopped
        1   T olive oil
    1/2   avocado, diced
            Salt and pepper to taste

Mix all ingredients, except avocado, in a large bowl. Right before serving, add avocado and stir gently, along with salt and pepper to taste. Great with chips or on grilled chicken.

Marinade for Flank Steak

Makes 1 1/4 cups

1/4 c soy sauce
3 T honey
2 T wine vinegar
1 1/2 t garlic powder
1 1/2 t ground ginger
3/4 c vegetable oil
1 green onion, chopped

Mix together soy sauce, honey and vinegar. Blend in garlic powder, ginger and oil. Add onion. Pour over meat and marinate for 4 hours or more.

Orange Cantonese Sauce (for ribs)

Makes 2 1/4 cups

1 c orange marmalade
1/2 c soy sauce
3/4 c water
1/2 t ground ginger
1/2 t garlic powder
Dash pepper

Combine all ingredients in bowl. Mix well. Pour over ribs before broiling or roasting.

Papaya Curry Marinade

Makes 1 cup

1 ripe papaya, peeled, seeded and sliced
1/2 c orange juice
1/4 c vegetable oil
2 T lemon juice
1 1/2 t curry powder
2 t salt

continued...

Combine all ingredients in blender or food processor and blend well. Spoon over meat and marinate overnight. Best used on poultry or pork.

Makes 4-6 cups

Pickled Cucumber

1 1/2 t salt
1 1/2 t pepper
1 1/2 t celery seed
   1 c sugar
  2/3 c vinegar
   4 cucumbers, peeled and thinly sliced
   1 lg onion, thinly sliced

Combine salt, pepper, celery seed, sugar and vinegar in a large bowl. Stir well until sugar is dissolved. Add cucumber and onions. Let sit at room temperature for 2 hours, stirring about every 20 minutes. Pack into pint jars. Cover tightly and refrigerate for at least two days.

Makes 4 cups

Veggie Trio Chutney

   1 cucumber, peeled, seeded and chopped
   3 ripe tomatoes, peeled, seeded and chopped
   1 Maui onion, cut in half and thinly sliced
   2 cloves garlic, finely chopped
  1/4 c Chinese parsley, chopped
  1/4 c fresh lime juice
   1 Hawaiian red chili pepper, seeded and chopped
    Salt and pepper to taste

Combine all ingredients; mix well. Chill.
Serve with seafood, hamburgers or tacos.

Kids' Cuisine

Kids' Cuisine

A Berry Good Banana Smoothie

2 ripe bananas
2 c fresh or frozen strawberries
1 c milk
1 c plain yogurt (may substitute flavored yogurt for variety)

Peel and slice the bananas. Wash and cut the tops of the strawberries. Put the fruit into the blender with the milk and yogurt. Blend until smooth and **WONDERFUL**.

A Cookie and a Kiss

A house should have a cookie jar
For when it's half past three
And children hurry home from school
As hungry as can be.
There's nothing quite so splendid
In filling children up
As spicy, fluffy ginger cakes
And sweet milk in a cup.

A house should have someone
Waiting with a hug
No matter what the child brings home
A puppy or a bug.
For children will only loiter
When the bell rings to dismiss
If no one's home to greet them
With a cookie and a kiss.

Chocolate Truffles

2 T cocoa powder
1/4 c powdered sugar
1/4 c cream cheese, softened
1/4 c nuts, chopped
Chocolate sprinkles

Combine first 4 ingredients in a bowl and form into small balls with hands. Pour sprinkles into a pie plate and roll chocolate balls in them. Chill on waxed paper at least 2 hours. **Serve & Share!**

Dirt Cake

2 sm pkgs instant vanilla pudding
2 c milk
8 oz Cool Whip
1/2 stick butter, softened
8 oz cream cheese, softened
1 c powdered sugar
1 pkg Oreo Cookies, crushed

Mix pudding with milk; blend in Cool Whip and set aside. Blend butter with cream cheese and powdered sugar until creamy. Combine pudding mixture with cream cheese mixture and mix well. Place in a container in the following layers: 1/3 Oreos, 1/2 creamy mixture, 1/3 Oreos, 1/2 creamy mixture. Top layer is Oreos. Chill for at least two hours. **Oh so yummy!**

Got Gak?

        1   c Elmer's glue
        1   c water

Combine and mix well. Set aside.

        1   T Borax
      1/2   c water
    15-20   drops food coloring of choice

Combine and mix well. Mix into glue mixture.
(This is not edible, but loads of fun!)

Makes 2 quarts

High Energy Fruit Mix

        2   c banana chips
        1   c dried apricots, cut in quarters
        1   c raisins
      1/2   c nuts (slivered almonds, cashews, walnuts or peanuts)
      1/2   c coconut flakes

Combine all ingredients in a large bowl. Mix with a wooden
spoon. Store in an airtight container or place mixture in sandwich bags
for school lunches.

Makes 9 cups

Island Style Party Mix (Furikake Mix)

1/2 c margarine
1/2 c light Karo Syrup
1/2 c vegetable oil
3 T shoyu
6 T sugar
2 lg boxes Crispix cereal
1 bottle Furikake (any style)

Preheat oven to 250°. Heat margarine, syrup, oil, shoyu and sugar over medium heat until sugar dissolves. Pour cereal into a large roasting pan. Pour the well-stirred syrup mixture over the cereal; mix well until cereal is evenly coated. Sprinkle with the furikake, mix well again. Bake for one hour, stirring after 30 minutes. Remove mix from oven and let it cool.

Store in an airtight container. *An Island-style snack to the max!*

Serves 6

Orange Slush

1 8oz can frozen orange juice
2 scoops vanilla ice cream
1 tray ice cubes
1 t vanilla extract

Put all ingredients in a blender. Process until smooth. Pour into chilled glasses and serve. *Oh, so refreshing!*

Party Potato Casserole

       1   can cream of celery soup
       1   sm onion, grated
       1   8oz pkg cream cheese, softened
     1/2   c milk
       1   32oz bag frozen hash browns
       1   lb cheddar cheese, grated
           Paprika

Preheat oven to 350°. Combine soup, onion, cream cheese and milk in a saucepan. Stir until cream cheese is melted. In a 9"x13" baking dish, layer 1/2 of hash browns and 1/2 of cheddar cheese. Pour cream cheese mixture over and repeat with layer of remaining hash browns and cheddar cheese.

Bake for one hour. Remove from oven and sprinkle with paprika. **Great for parties!**

Pizza Muffin

       1   English Muffin
       2   T prepared spaghetti sauce
       2   slices cheese (any type)

Preheat toaster oven to 350°. Split the English muffin into 2 halves. Spread 1 tablespoon of sauce on each muffin half. Top with a cheese slice. Warm muffin in toaster oven for several minutes. Then, top broil to melt cheese, about 1-2 minutes. **A yummy lunch idea!**

Play Dough To Eat

1/2 c peanut butter
1/4 c honey
1 c powdered milk

Mix peanut butter, honey and 1/2 cup powdered milk together. It's easiest if you use your hands. Add more dry powdered milk until it feels thick enough to mold. Roll out and cut with cookie cutters or shape into any form. Decorate with sprinkles, chocolate chips, cherries or whatever you like. **Have Fun!**

Puppy Chow

1 c peanut butter
6 oz semi sweet chocolate chips
1/2 c butter
1 lg box Crispix cereal
1 lb box powdered sugar

Combine first 3 ingredients in microwave-safe bowl. Microwave for 1 minute on high. Stir. Repeat until smooth. Place cereal in large bowl with lid. Pour chocolate mixture over cereal, close lid and shake well. Refrigerate until firm, approximately 2 hours. Break mixture into small pieces. Add powdered sugar and toss until well-coated. Looks like puppy chow! **Eat & Enjoy!**

Refreshing Fruit Pizza

1   15oz can pineapple chunks
3   bananas, sliced
1   15oz pkg sugar cookie dough
1   c whipped topping, custard or vanilla pudding
1   10 1/2oz can mandarin oranges, drained
2   c fresh strawberries, sliced
1/2   c cherry pie filling
1   kiwi fruit, sliced

Preheat oven to 375°. Drain pineapple juice from pineapple chunks into a small bowl. Place banana into juice; set aside. Lightly grease a 12-inch pizza pan. Press cookie dough into pizza pan, about 1/8-inch thick. Bake 12-15 minutes until edges begin to brown. Cool.

Spread whipped topping over cooled cookie dough crust. Drain juice from bananas. Arrange fruit in circles on topping, working from outside toward center. Refrigerate until served. Create your own fresh fruit combinations. *Colorful & Wonderful!*

Yummy and Nutty Energy Bars

     2   c Quaker Oats, old fashioned
     1   c unsalted peanuts
     1   c raisins
   1/2   c sunflower seeds
 2 1/2   c Rice Krispies
   1/2   c butter
   1/2   c chunky peanut butter
     1   10oz pkg marshmallows
     2   T sesame seeds

Preheat oven to 250°. Toast oats in pan in oven for 15 minutes. Remove pan. Add peanuts, raisins and sunflower seeds to oats and mix together. When slightly cooled, fold in Rice Krispies. Set mixture aside.

In a large pot melt butter, peanut butter and marshmallows, blending well. When slightly cooled, add dry ingredients. Put mixture into 9"x13" pan and sprinkle with sesame seeds. Use wax paper or Saran Wrap to firmly press the mixture flat.

Cool completely. Cut into candy sized pieces.

INDEX

Breads & Breakfast

Starters

Soups, Salads & Dressings

Vegetables & Side Dishes

Entrées

Chicken —

Desserts

Marinades & Sauces

Kids' Cuisine

808-228-5900

2 C mango
1 c red bell pepper
2/3c green onion
1/4 c cilantro
2 T lime juice
4 T olive oil

3 T Bals.
2 T lemon juice
1 T Dijon
2 garlic
1/2 C olive oil